Dante | Hafiz

DANTE | HAFIZ
Readings on the Sigh, the Gaze, and Beauty

Franco Masciandaro
Peter Booth

Edited by
Nicola Masciandaro & Öykü Tekten

KAF
PRESS

Dante | Hafiz: Readings on the Sigh, the Gaze, and Beauty
© the authors
2017

KAF Press
http://www.kafcollective.com

Cover image: Hilma af Klint, *The Swan*, nr 18, Group 9,
1915. Public domain image. Source:
https://commons.wikimedia.org/wiki/File:Hilma_Af_Klin
t_-_1915_-_The_Swan,_No._18.jpg

ISBN-13: 978-0692887486 (KAF)
ISBN-10: 0692887482

CONTENTS

I. SIGH

II. GAZE

III. BEAUTY

MIRACLE OF THE SIGH

Nicola Masciandaro

Beyond the sphere that circles widest / passes the sigh that issues from my heart.

– Dante

Beyond the sphere passeth the arrow of our sigh. Hafiz! Be silent.

– Hafiz

Flowing between life and breath, suspended inside voice and word, flying the bonds of desire and the bounds of thought, pre-living the fleeting moment of death—is there anything a sigh cannot touch, nothing its arrow will not pierce? At once phenomenon and figure, the sigh is both a companion to all expression and a secret language unto itself. "And my thick sighs a mystick language prove, / Unknown to all but me and him I love" (Herman Hugo, *Pia desideria*). So, if the love of poetry and the poetry of love are unthinkable if not impossible without the sigh, perhaps this follows not only from the necessity of sighing to our biological and psychological life (as per recent neuroscientific research), but from a greater mystery and universal truth of sighing itself. For medieval poets and mystics, the sigh of the human heart, an "innate passion of the soul proceeding from a suspension or hovering of spirit [*Suspirium est passio anime innata ex spiritum suspensio*]" (Boncompagno da Signa, *Rota Veneris*), might traverse the cosmos and communicate with its Creator, the divine Reality whose love, as Ibn Arabi held, is "in actual fact the Sigh of God Himself epiphanized in beings and yearning to return to Himself" (Henry Corbin, *Alone with the Alone*).

In its universality, the sigh is a form of the oneness of life and thus also the proper term and actual medium of the spiritual unity of human beings. As Meher Baba said in 1933, on Easter Sunday at a chapel in Portofino, "The sigh within the prayer is the same in the heart of the Christian, the Mohammedan, or the Jew." Nowadays, in this narrow upside down world suspended within an always darker and vaster universe, it might seem that our sighs have nowhere to go. As Cioran wrote in *A Short History of Decay*, "We perceive no more of Creation than its destitution, the grim reality . . . a lonely universe before a lonely heart, each predestined to disjoin and to exasperate each other in the antithesis." Or is such a view only the too-common cowardice, a shrinking of the heart before what Kierkegaard calls "This . . . road we all must walk—over the bridge of sighs into eternity"? Has the universe really expanded, or is it only the human sigh—*your* sigh—which has shrunk? Either way, it is best to follow the words of Muhammad Iqbal, whose Dante-inspired masterpiece *Javid Nama* [Pilgrimage of Eternity] takes the path of the poet's "peregrino spirito" [pilgrim spirit] through the spheres: *I am a sigh, I will mount to the heavens!*

*

If I sigh for the miraculous, for the beauty that takes breath away in wonder, maybe it is because the sigh itself is a miracle. And if it is not, if as the song says, a sigh is just a sigh, perhaps that *is* the miracle, that a sigh, to be miraculous, need not be anything other than itself.

The miracle of this gathering is that we get to hear and speak the sighs of Dante and Hafiz together, to have them, side by side, in the same room.

Dante died in 1321. Hafiz was born in 1325. So this is something that could never have happened. Or, in light of the mystery of reincarnation, properly identified by one anonymous author as "in no way a theory which one has to believe or not believe . . . a fact which is [to be] either known through experience or ignored" (*Meditations on the Tarot*), this may be something that could never have not happened. Thus who knows, this gathering might be both and something better than either, the miracle of a third thing, the event of the presence of one in whose name two or three gather.

The impossible is inevitable. And in this case, there is also lightning, a striking resemblance. Above all, the greatness of these two poets, the height and depth of their sighs, belongs to the sphere of intense experience, ecstatic and torturous, of the intersection of human and divine love, more specifically, the noble love of a woman and the love of God. For Dante, it was the death of Beatrice which marked the center of his poetry's turning toward the divine. Only from the abyss of sorrow and the poet's death to himself within it does there spring the miraculous vision of the *Commedia*, the potentiality of a truly new poetry, of a word that authentically writes itself now, in light of the eternal present. As Dante states near the end of the *Vita Nuova*, "And to arrive at that, I apply myself as much as I can, as she truly knows. So that, if it be pleasing to Him for whom all things live that my life may last for some years, I hope to say of her what was never said of any other woman." For Hafiz, the death of his beloved instead takes place virtually, in experience, upon the imminence of the long-sought moment when he could finally realize his desire. Where the death of Dante's beloved is the ground of seeking her in God, Hafiz's earthly love is eclipsed by desire for the divinity that grants him the opportunity to fulfil that love. With uncanny complementarity, the two poets' experiences appear as different as they are similar. Hafiz's story is recounted by Meher Baba as follows:

> Once in his youth, Hafiz encountered a very beautiful girl of a wealthy family. That very instant he fell in love with her; it was not in the carnal way, but he loved her beauty. At the same time, he was in contact with his Spiritual Master, Attar . . . Hafiz, being Attar's disciple, used to visit him daily for years. He used to compose a ghazal a day and sing it to Attar . . . Twenty years passed and all this time Hafiz was full of the fire of love for the beautiful woman, and he loved his Master,

too. Once, Attar asked him: "Tell me what you want." Hafiz expressed how he longed for the woman. Attar replied: "Wait, you will have her." Ten more years passed by, thirty in all, and Hafiz became desperate and disheartened . . . Hafiz blazed out: "What have I gained by being with you? Thirty years have gone by!" Attar answered: "Wait, you will know one day." . . . Hafiz performed *chilla-nashini,* that is, he sat still within the radius of a drawn circle for 40 days to secure fulfillment of his desire. It is virtually impossible for one to sit still for 40 days within the limits of a circle. But Hafiz's love was so great that it did not matter to him. On the fortieth day, an angel appeared before him and looking at the angel's beauty, Hafiz thought: "What is that woman's beauty in comparison with this heavenly splendor!" The angel asked what he desired. Hafiz replied that he be able to wait on the pleasure of his Master's wish. At four o'clock on the morning of the last day, Hafiz . . . went to his Master who embraced him. In that embrace, Hafiz became God-conscious. (*Lord Meher*)

Following love's infinity in the face of the finite, through the domain of death, the poetry of Dante and Hafiz fills the space traversed by *longing,* the degree or mode of love which moves between desire and surrender, the form of eros that at once insists on satisfaction and grasps the futility of that insistence. As the word of the word of love, the tongueless articulation of the heart before and after speech, a murmuring of the heart as mouth around the spiritual limits of language, the sigh is the proper expression of longing, of desire across distance and the hopelessness of separation. Thus the sphere-piercing spatiality of the sigh, its mapping of the paradoxical parameters of the heart as something both excluded from and already established within its own home. Like a breath at the edge of the universe which is no less one's own, the sigh traces the heart as no less exterior than interior, as both trapped within and containing what holds it. Augustine defines the heart as "where I am whoever or whatever I am [*ubi ego sum quicumque sum*]" and love as "my weight [which] bears me wheresoever I am borne [*pondus meum, amor meus; eo feror, quocumque feror*]" (Augustine, *Confessions*). So the sigh, echoing simultaneously one's first and last breath, both the spirit which animates you in the first place and the expiration which becomes no longer yours, pertains to an essential openness and mobility, the unbounded wherever and wheresoever of things.

This for me is the sigh's miracle—not anything supernatural, but that it marks the miracle of reality itself as infinitely open, as spontaneously expanding without limit or horizon into more and more of itself. Hear how, on the one hand, a sigh resonates with the sense of the weight of facticity and necessity, the crushing gravity of *that* (that things are as they are, that anything is, that something is not) and hear, on the other hand, how a sigh floats in the space *between* the actual and the ideal, in the sky of its own indetermination and freedom. The suspension of the sigh, its hovering, pertains to the paradox of freedom as realizable yet unpossessable, the necessity of freeing oneself from oneself, from one's own freedom, in order to be free. As Meister Eckart says, "The just man serves neither God nor creatures, for he is free, . . . and the closer he is to freedom . . . the more he is freedom itself." The sigh is the dialetheia of freedom and necessity, the joy (and sorrow) of knowing that nothing is fixed and the sorrow (and joy) of seeing that everything is—that thank God there is absolutely nothing and everything *you* can do about it. As Vernon Howard said, referring to yourself, "you want to take *that* to Heaven?"

The admixture of joy and sorrow found in the sigh reflects the miraculous fact, the light weight and grave lightness, of reality's paradoxical openness. As Agamben says in *The Coming Community*, "The root of all pure joy and sadness is that the world is as it is." The intimacy with separation spoken in the sigh likewise manifests separation as a special order of intimacy. As Mechthild of Magdeburg, a Beguine of the 13th century says, "O blissful distance from

God, how lovingly am I connected with you!" Or as Meher Baba once spontaneously rhymed, "Oh, you ignorant, all-knowing Soul / what a plight you are in! / Oh, you weak, all-powerful Soul / what a plight you are in! / Oh, you miserable, all-happy Soul / what a plight you are in! / What a plight! / What a sight! / What a delight!" (*Lord Meher*).

We are indeed in a fiX, in a spot marked by a great, unfathomable X. Such is the order of the truth of the sigh. That the mystery of the world is more than metaphysical. That not only is there something rather than nothing, but that one is. That there is not only eternity but time, not only good but evil, not only truth but illusion, not only oneness but separation, not only the universe but the individual, not only you but me. These are astonishing things, stupendous facts pointing to a reality more stupendous still. All is somehow more infinite for being finite. In other words, there is something about the sigh that turns everything inside out. I hear Levinas sighing as he writes, "Time is not the limitation of being but its relationship with infinity. Death is not annihilation but the question that is necessary for this relationship with infinity, or time, to be produced."

The opening of the world, in both senses, is poetry, the miracle of the word which takes you aside and makes one hear its silence and speak what one cannot say. Thus the singular story in the Gospel of Mark of Jesus's sigh: "And they brought to him a man who was deaf and had an impediment in his speech; and they besought him to lay his hand upon him. And taking him aside from the multitude private, he put his fingers into his ears, and spat and touched his tongue; and looking up to heaven, he sighed, and said to him, 'Ephphatha,' that is, 'Be opened.' And his ears were opened, his tongue was released, and he spoke plainly" (Mark 7:31-4).

Therefore, to close my opening of this gathering, to thank the sigh for making possible our being side by side with these two poets, I will read a poem by a third poet, one Pseudo-Leopardi, on the same theme, from *Cantos for the Crestfallen*:

Unable to swim the ocean of each other's eyes
We must sit side by side, gazing at a blind world
Whose dumb mouth has lost all taste for silence.

Heads dizzy as ours naturally lean together,
Kept from falling off only by the golden sighs
Suspending these bodies like puppet strings.

The soft tautness of the secret lines is thinning us,
Sweetly drawing all life-feeling inward and up
Into something pulling strongly from far above.

There is no doubt that the sigh-threads will one day
Draw our hearts right through the tops of our heads,
Eventually turning everything totally inside out.

Already my body is something much less my own,
As if the thought of your form is my new skeleton
And your memory of my flesh your new strength.

If I embrace you my own power would crush me
And if you cling to me I would surely evaporate.
Dying lovers do not touch without touching suicide.

Side by side we float and stand. It is our way of lying
Bound together across space on this lost world
Whose eyes will not survive seeing us face to face.

Dante's Sighs/Sigh

Franco Masciandaro

I

I would like to begin by changing the title of my talk to "Dante's Sighs/Sigh," thus announcing the plurality of sighs encountered in the texts I have selected—from Dante's early work, *Vita Nuova (New Life)*, and from the more widely known, *The Divine Comedy*—and at the same time introducing the unique, singular sigh, the one defined by Nicola as "the sigh of the human heart," which "might traverse the cosmos and communicate with its Creator, the divine Reality whose love . . . in actual fact [is] the Sigh of God Himself epiphanized in beings and yearning to return to Himself." Thus, the sigh in and *of* poetry, that we will in a moment find exemplified in Dante's works, is profoundly and mysteriously bound to the *archè,* the beginning of all beginnings of all acts of creation, as represented in the first scene of Genesis:

> In the beginning God created the heavens and the earth. Now the earth was a formless void, there was darkness over the deep, and God's spirit hovered over the water.

We may think of God's "spirit hovered over the water" as His breath or sigh preceding and announcing the act of creation by the power of His words: "God said, 'Let there be light' and there was light," etcetera.

Similarly, as Nicola spoke of the sigh as "both a companion to all expression and a secret language unto itself," the sigh, like the gaze, the smile, the voice, or tears, is at once *before* and *beyond* language, that is, before and beyond discursive reasoning, like silent prayer, or like music, especially—in the words of T.S. Eliot from the third of his *Four Quartets* ("The Dry Salvages")—"music heard so deeply / that it is not heard at all, but you are the music / while the music lasts." I like to think of music as one extended, infinite sigh, including the music of poetry, as Dante spoke of in his *De vulgari eloquentia (The Eloquence of the Vernacular,* II.v.2), defining it as *fictio rhetorica musicaque poita* (rhetorical fiction made with music).

As we shall see, the one and the many sighs, are at once distinct and yet profoundly interconnected. For example, a sigh of despair that we find in *Inferno,* as it expresses the negation of hope, it also recalls it, points to it, and in a sense affirms it, as the shadow at once negates and points to light. To cite another example, a sigh of nostalgia for a past, lost happy time may hide a sigh of longing for a future and even transcendent happiness, one belonging to the eternal now of the celestial paradise.

It is now time to turn our attention to some unique moments in Dante's *New Life* and later in *The Divine Comedy,* in which the figure of the sigh stands out as a sign of heightened creativity that—to use an Italian expression—seems "to burn through the page."

We encounter the first example of the figure of the sigh, in the *New Life,* in the episode of Dante's departure from his city (i.e., Florence, whose name is never mentioned in this work, perhaps to suggest the universality of the city, that is, a *civitas* that is at once Florence and just a city), a departure which causes him to experience the loss of the presence, and especially the greeting of the beloved Beatrice. We should recall that earlier in the *New Life* (III.1-2) Dante had written:

> Poi che fuoro passati tanti die, che appunto erano compiuti li nove anni appresso l'apparimento soprascritto di questa gentilissima, ne l'ultimo di questi die avvenne che questa mirabile donna apparve a me vestita di colore bianchissimo, in mezzo a due gentili donne, le quali erano di più

lunga etade; e passando per una via, volse li occhi
verso quella parte ov'io era molto pauroso, e per
la sua ineffabile cortesia, la quale è oggi meritata
nel grande secolo, mi salutoe molto
virtuosamente, tanto che me parve allora vedere
li termini de la mia beatitudine.

After many days had passed, so that precisely
nine years were completed following the
appearance described above of this most gentle
lady, it happened that on the last of these days
this marvelous lady appeared to me dressed in
purest white, between two gentle ladies who were
of greater years; and passing along a street, she
turned her eyes to that place where I stood in
great fear, and in her ineffable courtesy, which
today is awarded in life everlasting, she greeted
me with exceeding virtue, such that I then
seemed to see all the terms of beatitude.[1]

This retrospective glance at the scene of the power of
Beatrice's greeting and its extraordinary effect on Dante
poet and lover helps us to find deeper meaning and deeper
resonances in the episode of Dante's sighing for what he
considers the loss of his beatitude, as he travels away from
his city and from Beatrice:

Appresso la morte di questa donna alquanti die
avvenne cosa per la quale me convenne partire de
la sopradetta cittade e ire verso quelle parti
dov'era la gentile donna ch'era stata mia difesa,
avvegna che non tanto fosse lontano lo termine
de lo mio andare quanto ella era. E tutto ch'io
fosse a la compagnia di molti quanto a la vista,
l'andare mi dispiacea sì, che quasi li sospiri non
poteano disfogare l'angoscia che lo cuore sentia,

---

[1] All quotations in English from *Vita Nuova* are from Dante
Alighieri, *Vita Nuova*, trans. Dino S. Cervigni and Edward Vasta
(Notre Dame: University of Notre Dame Press, 1995).

però ch'io mi dilungava de la mia beatitudine. E però lo dolcissimo segnore, lo quale mi segnoreggiava per la vertù de la gentilissima donna, ne la mia imaginazione apparve come peregrino leggeramente vestito e di vili drappi. Elli mi parea disbigottito, e guardava la terra, salvo che talora li suoi occhi mi parea che si volgessero ad uno fiume bello e corrente e chiarissimo, lo quale sen gia lungo questo cammino là ov'io era. (*Vita Nuova* IX.1-4)

A few days after the death of this lady something happened that made it necessary for me to leave the aforementioned city and travel toward those parts where was the gentle lady who had been my defense, although the destination of my journey was not so distant as she was. And although, to all appearances, I kept company with many, the journey so displeased me that my sighs could hardly relieve the anguish that my heart felt, because I was distancing myself from my beatitude. Therefore, the sweetest Lord, who ruled me through the power of the most gentle lady, appeared in my imagination as a pilgrim dressed meagerly and in simple vestments. He seemed to me frightened, and he stared at the ground, except that at times his eyes seemed to turn toward a river, beautiful and swift and utterly clear, that flowed along the road there where I was.

The motif of absence, to which the figure of the sigh is connected, is announced by Dante's reference to the death of a gentle lady, whom he once had seen in the company of Beatrice—as we learn in the preceding chapter—with death being universally acknowledged as the extreme, irreparable cause of human beings' absence from the journey of this life. There is also an underlying intimation that, analogously, the distance now separating Dante from the beloved Beatrice will one day also coincide with the absence brought about by death, for we recall that earlier we read that Beatrice's "courtesy . . . today is awarded in life everlasting." We should also note that Dante's sighs, which fail to relieve his anguish caused by the distance that now separates him from Beatrice's greeting, with its power to bestow upon him beatitude or blessedness, constitute the expression, or language of that anguish, which is equivalent to what tears are to grief. Significantly, as they fail, they at once express Dante's longing to be again in the presence of the beloved, to again receive the gift of her saving greeting, both in time, in the journey of this life, and beyond time, for the deeper meaning of beatitude, or salvation, is expressed, as we learn at the beginning of the *New Life* (III.4), by the Italian word *saluto* (greeting) being akin to the word *salute* (salvation, in theological terms). Hence, we can speak at once of Dante's sighs as a longing for or a nostalgia for the past event of Beatrice's salvific greeting, within time, as well as a nostalgia for the future beatitude that after death, in the eternal now of "life everlasting," Beatrice can still bestow on Dante.

Another significant expression, indeed a dramatization of this double nostalgia is offered to us by the figure of Love (the fictional god of Love) as a pilgrim who appears in Dante's imagination. The pilgrim, as Dante, later in the *New Life*, will define at some length, experiences at once the nostalgia for the home he has left behind as well as the longing, or nostalgia for the sacred place, or spiritual home he hopes to reach—whether Santiago de Compostela, in Galicia, or Rome, or Jerusalem. Dante's pilgrim appears in his (and our own) imagination as a frightened, sad figure, who gazes with downcast eyes at the ground but also, at times, turns his eyes to a "beautiful . . . and utterly clear river," which—as a *locus amoenus*, the beautiful place of literary tradition—signals the presence, and correspondingly, the longing or nostalgia for the Garden of Eden before the Fall as well as for the Celestial Garden that it foreshadows. I should point out that the episode we are examining ends with a sonnet in which it is the pilgrim who sighs, clearly revealing, as Dante's poetic intuition, a projection and dramatic representation of his own sighs, with emphasis on anguish or on the nostalgia for the past, as no mention is made of the paradisiacal scene evoked by the beautiful river:

Cavalcando l'altr'ier per un cammino
pensoso de l'andar che mi sgradia,
trovai Amore in mezzo de la via
in abito leggier di peregrino.
Ne la sembianzia mi parea meschino,
Come avesse perduto segnoria;
E sospirando pensoso venia,
Per non veder la gente a capo chino . . .

Riding the other day along a road,
musing upon the journey that I disliked,
I met Love in the middle of the way
in meager dress of a pilgrim.
In his aspect he seemed to me poor,
as if he had lost his lordship;
and sighing he came pensively,
head down in order not to see the people . . .

Before turning our attention to another example of the creative moment marked by the presence of the figure of the sigh in the *New Life*, I must cite a passage from the beginning of the second chapter following the one we have just discussed (X.1), in which Dante describes again, in a new light, the salvific power of Beatrice's greeting—a description which follows that of his beloved's denial of her greeting, in response to "excessive vicious voices that appeared to defame [him] viciously," because of his feigned love expressed for the so called "screen lady" in other to deflect attention from his love of Beatrice, and thus protecting it from those vulgar slanderers who remind us of the *lausengiers* in the courtly love poetry of Provence:

Dico che quando ella appario da parte alcuna, per
la speranza de la mirabile salute nullo nemico mi
rimanea, anzi mi giugnea una fiamma di caritade,
la quale mi facea perdonare a chiunque m'avesse

offeso; e chi allora m'avesse domandato di cosa alcuna, la mia risponsione sarebbe stata solamente "Amore", con viso vestito d'umilitade.

I say that when she appeared from any direction, in the hope of her miraculous greeting I was left with no enemy, but rather there arose in me a flame of charity that made me forgive whoever might have offended me; and if anyone had then asked me anything, my answer would have been only "Love," with a countenance clothed in humility.

In light of these inspiring and deeply moving words we now gain a deeper understanding of the depth of Dante's sighs of anguish, first as we found in the episode of his departure from his city and his beloved, and then in the episode of his loss of what he deemed to be, in his words, the source of "all [his] beatitude." However, as the reader soon discovers, this loss of Beatrice's greeting turns out to be providential, as Dante soon discovers a salutary new way of experiencing the beatitude once conferred to him by his beloved's greeting by singing her praises and directing them not only to Beatrice, but to a larger audience—a community of ladies endowed with a noble heart, a *cor gentil*, beginning with a chorus of those ladies whom he addresses with the words of the famous *canzone*, *Donne ch'avete intelletto d'amore (Ladies who have understanding of love)*, which marks the beginning of a new poetics, the poetics of praise (la poetica della lode). We may discover a small measure of the larger economy of the salvific power of Beatrice's greeting or mere presence, which transcends the earlier narrow economy whereby her greeting was defined only for its power to confer beatitude mainly on Dante, reading the following excerpt extracted from this complex, rich *canzone*:

Madonna è disiata in sommo cielo:
or voi di sua virtù farvi savere.
Dico, qual vuol gentil donna parere

vada con lei, che quando va per via,
gitta nei cor villani Amore un gelo,
per che onne lor pensero agghiaccia e pere;
e qual soffrisse di starla a vedere
diverria nobil cosa, o si morria.
E quando trova alcun che degno sia
di veder lei, quei prova sua vertute,
ché li avvien, ciò che li dona, in salute,
e sì l'umilia, ch'ogni offesa oblia.
Ancor l'ha Dio per maggior grazia dato
che non pò mal finir chi l'ha parlato.

The lady is desired in highest heaven:
now I wish to have you know of her virtue.
I say, let who wishes to appear a gentle lady
go with her, for when she goes along the way,
into villainous hearts Love casts a chill,
whereby all their thoughts freeze and perish;
and who might suffer to stay and behold her
would change into a noble thing, or die.
And when she finds someone worthy
to behold her, he experiences her power,
for what she gives him turns into salvation,
and so humbles him that he forgets every offense.
God has given her an even greater grace:
that one cannot end in evil who has spoken to her.

The larger economy of salvation we spoke of now clearly reveals the intersection of two perspectives, human and divine, and therefore, close to our concern, we now perceive foreshadows of a new direction of Dante's sighs.

After writing several sonnets in praise of Beatrice, reaching a wider audience in his city, and after recalling the death of Beatrice's father, writing that he "to eternal glory passed truly," for he "was good in a high degree," Dante narrates how, seized by illness, and meditating on life's fleeting duration, he "began to weep . . . over such misery. Hence, sighing heavily," he said within himself: "Of necessity it must happen that the most gentle Beatrice one day will die" (XXIII.1-4). Here Dante's heavy sighing,

16

together with the silent language of tears, expresses much more than the anguish that earlier—as we have noted—Dante felt for the distance separating him from Beatrice, and therefore, implicitly, his longing to be again in her presence and again experience the beatitude of her salvific greeting. This sighing is a sign of the fundamental, absolute fear of death, that Dante shares with all human beings. As a "statement," or "assertion" Dante's sighing and tears implicitly demand an answer, or counter-assertion that may help him accept, and perhaps acquire a new knowledge of the universal tragic condition of life ending in death. In dramatistic terms we may say with Kenneth Burke,

> Stated broadly the dialectical (agonistic) approach to knowledge is through the act of assertion, whereby one "suffers" the kind of knowledge that is the reciprocal of his act. This is the process embodied in tragedy, where the agent's action involves an understanding of the act, an understanding that transcends the act. The act, in being an assertion, has called forth a counter-assertion in the elements that compose its context. And when the agent is enabled to see in terms of this counter-assertion, he has transcended the space that characterized him at the start. In this final stage of tragic vision, intrinsic and extrinsic motivations are merged.[2]

Dante (and his reader) finds a counter-assertion that provides an "answer" to his sighing and his tears in the drama that is played out in his imagination. For brevity's sake I shall read only the translation of this drama:

> At the outset of the wandering that my fantasy took to, there appeared to me certain faces of disheveled women, who said to me: "You, too, will die"; then, following these ladies, there

---

[2] Kenneth Burke, *A Grammar of Motives* (New York: George Braziller, 1945), 38-39.

appeared certain faces strange and horrible to look at, which said to me "You are dead." Thus, my fantasy beginning to wander, I reached a point at which I knew not where I was; and I seemed to see women roaming disheveled, crying along the way, wondrously sad; and I seemed to see the sun darken, so that stars appeared of a color that made me think that they wept; and it seemed to me that birds flying through the air fell dead, and there were tremendous earthquakes. And marveling in that fantasy, and terribly afraid, I imagined that a friend came to me to say: "Don't you know yet? Your wonderful lady has departed from this world." With that I began to weep most piteously; and I wept not only in my imagination, but I wept with my eyes, bathing them in true tears. I imagined myself looking toward heaven, and I seemed to see multitudes of angels who were returning upward, and they had before them a small cloud of purest white. It seemed to me that these angels sang gloriously, and the words I seemed to hear of their song were these: *Osanna in exelcis* [glory in the highest]; and nothing else I seemed to hear. Then it seemed to me that my heart, where was much love, said to me: "It is true that dead lies our lady." And with that I seemed to go and see the body in which had dwelled that most noble and blessed soul; and so strong was the erroneous fantasy that it showed me that lady dead; and it seemed that women covered her—that is, her head—with a white vail; and it appeared that her face had so much the aspect of humility that she seemed to say: "I am beholding the font of peace." In this imagining I felt such humility at seeing her that I summed Death, and said: "Sweet Death, come to me, and be not unkind, for you must be noble; in such a place have you been! Now come to me, I greatly desire you, as you can see, for I already wear your color."

As we pause to reflect on this dramatic representation that takes place in Dante's imagination, or fantasy, which has also been characterized as a vision, we note that clearly it plays out the opposition between Dante's fear of death, his own and, especially, the death of Beatrice, and a new, unforeseen answer, or, in Burkean terms, counter-assertion, whereby the death of Beatrice, with the earthquake and the darkening of the sun that come with it, is represented as analogous to the death of Christ—a death that is both tragic, as attested by His cry on the Cross, *Elì, Elì, lama asabthani (My God, my God, why have you abandoned me?),* and has the power to save humankind, conquering death with His Resurrection. We should note that this imagined death of Beatrice, accompanied by multitudes of angels returning to Heaven, following a "cloud of purest white," resembles more an ascension (like Christ's) than a death. Equally important to note is the creative power, although hidden and unforeseen, of Dante's sighing, accompanied by tears and their unique language, which called forth the "answer," or "counter-assertion" that we have commented on, including the "answer" to his anguish as he feared his own and Beatrice's death—an answer played out in the scene of Dante's desiring "Sweet Death."

After the death of Beatrice, foreshadowed by this vision, we find many examples of Dante's creative intuition underlying the representations of his sighs. For economy's sake I shall turn my attention to the episode in which Dante recalls seeing pilgrims who, coming from afar on their way to Rome, cross his city:

At the time when many folk go to see that blessed image that Jesus Christ left to us as a likeness of his most beautiful countenance, which my lady sees in glory, it happened that some pilgrims passed through a street that is like the middle of the city where was born, lived, and died the most gentle lady. These pilgrims were going, as it seemed to me, most pensively; therefore,

19

thinking of them, I said within myself: "These pilgrims seem to me from a faraway place, and I do not believe that they have ever heard speak of this lady, and know nothing of her; rather, their thoughts are on other things than these here, because they perhaps think about their distant friends, whom we do not know." [. . .] I said within myself: "If I could detain them awhile, I would nevertheless make them weep before they left this city, because I would speak words that would make anyone weep who heard them." Therefore, after they had passed from sight, I resolved to write a sonnet in which I would manifest what I had said within myself; and so that it would appear all the more moving, I resolved to write as if I had spoken to them; and I wrote this sonnet, which begins: *Oh pilgrims, who go along in thought* (XL).

As we read this passage, we find deep resonances that remind us of the first example of Dante's sigh in the *New Life*, which we have encountered, the sigh as a sign of his anguish for traveling away from his city and his beloved Beatrice, missing her salvific greeting. We recall that in that episode the god of Love appeared in Dante's imagination as a pilgrim, dressed meagerly and with downcast eyes. We also recall that in the sonnet inscribed in that episode it is the pilgrim who is represented as one who, "sighing . . . came pensively," clearly a projection or dramatis persona of Dante. In the pilgrims encountered by Dante, who "were going. . . most pensively" we also now find reverberations of the motif of the nostalgia for the friends they left behind, but also, implicitly, the nostalgia for the future, as they travel toward Rome, where they will see Christ's image, known as the *Veronica,* or *True Icon.* Significantly, now Dante wishes to share with these pilgrims, these strangers, both the anguish for the city's and his loss of Beatrice, as well as the longing to see her as a *figura Christi,* that is, one who, by analogy, resembles and points to Christ, Whom, as a blessed soul, she now sees face to face.

As we turn our attention to the sonnet addressed to the pilgrims, we find, again, in Dante's sighs an important measure of its creative power, that is, the power to move us, whereby the poet longs to move the pilgrims (XL):

> Oh pilgrims who go along in thought,
> Perhaps of something not present to you,
> do you come from such distant folk,
> as by your appearance you show us,
> that you weep not when you pass
> through the center of the sorrowing city,
> like those people who nothing,
> it seems, could comprehend of its pain?
> If you would linger to hear of it,
> surely the heart of many sighs tells me
> that in tears would you then part from here.
> The city has lost its *beatrice*;
> and the words that one may say of her
> have the power to make one cry.

We must not fail to note that in this sonnet, which, as it is related to the narrative inscribed in the prose that precedes it, constitutes, as a lyric, a form of perfecting and transcending of that prose, the unique creative power that informs it is manifested—as a kind of epiphany—in the image or figure of the poet's "heart of many sighs," which, like the god of Love and ultimately God Who Is Love (Deus caritas est), "tells," *dictates* to the poet, as Dante will tell the minor poet, Bonagiunta Orbicciani da Lucca, in *Purgatorio* XXIV.52-54:

> " . . . I' mi son un che, quando
> Amor mi spira, noto, e a quel modo
> ch'e' ditta dentro vo significando."

" . . . I am one who, when Love breaths
in me, takes note: what He, within, dictates,
I, in that way, without, would speak and shape."[3]

It cannot escape our attention the kinship suggested by the correspondences between the sighs of the heart in the *New Life* that "tell" the poet what to say to the pilgrims, in order to move them to tears, and the "spirar," or "breathing" revealed in   this purgatorial scene. As noted earlier, this sigh, this breathing precedes and transcends language, but it also constitutes its secret, unfathomable creative spark.

We shall now turn our attention to the last example of Dante's sigh, which we find in the chapter immediately following the one we have just discussed, the one containing the famous sonnet, whose opening verse Nicola cited epigraphically—*Oltre la spera che più larga gira (Beyond the sphere that circles widest):*

The sonnet that I . . . wrote begins: *Beyond the sphere;* it has in it five parts. In the first I tell where my thought goes, naming it by the name of one of its effects. In the second I say why it ascends on high: that is, who makes it go thus. In the third I tell what I saw: namely, a lady honored up above; and I call it then "pilgrim spirit," since it ascends on high spiritually, and like a pilgrim who is outside his fatherland, there abides. In the fourth I say that it sees her such, that is, in such a quality that I cannot understand it: that is to say that my thought ascends, in contemplating the quality of her, to a degree that my intellect cannot comprehend; for our intellect is to those blessed souls just as a weak eye is to the sun; and this the Philosopher says in the second book of the Metaphysics. In the fifth I say that, although I

---

[3] All quotations from Dante's poem are from *The Divine Comedy of Dante Alighieri*, 3 vols., trans, introduction and commentary by Allen Mandelbaum (Berkeley: University of California Press, 1982).

22

cannot understand that to which my thought takes me, namely, to her wonderful quality, this at least I understand, that all such thinking is about my lady, because I often hear her name in my thought; and at the end of this fifth part I say "dear my ladies," to make it clear they are ladies to whom I speak.

As we read the sonnet, we are struck by the transformation of key terms mentioned in the prose, which call forth our careful analysis or commentary:

Oltre la spera che più larga gira
Passa 'l sospiro ch'esce del mio cuore:
intelligenza nova, che l'Amore
piangendo mette in lui, pur su lo tira.
Quand'elli è giunto là dove disira,
vede donna, che riceve onore,
e luce sì, che per lo suo splendore
lo peregrino spirito la mira.
Vedela tal, che quando 'l mi ridice,
Io no lo intendo, sì parla sottile
al cor dolente, che lo fa parlare.
So io che parla di quella gentile,
Però che spesso ricorda Beatrice,
Sì ch'io lo 'ntendo ben, donne mie care.

Beyond the sphere that circles widest
penetrates the sigh that issues from my heart:
a new intelligence, which Love,
weeping, places in him, draws him ever upward.
When he arrives where he desires,
He sees a lady, who receives honor,
And so shines that, because of her splendor,
the pilgrim spirit gazes upon her,
He sees her such that when he tells me of it,
I do not understand him, so subtly does he speak
to the sorrowing heart, which makes him speak.
I know that he speaks of that gentle one,

23

for he often remembers Beatrice,
so that I understand him well, dear ladies.

A close reading will reveal a process of transformation of a key term, introduced in the prose, namely of Dante's thought: first into the figure of the "sigh" and then in the "new intelligence," placed in it by the weeping "Love" as a Prime Mover; and then in the figure of the "pilgrim spirit." The familiar, conventional opposition between thought, and hence discursive reason, language, on one hand, and the unique language of the sigh, on the other hand, is here transcended by virtue of a kind of symbiosis. It seems to me that the key word here is, indeed, transcendence, which at first, in Dante's journey, has been marked by a nostalgia for a beatitude promised by Beatrice's greeting in a horizontal, temporal dimension; and later, especially toward the end of the *New Life*, this transcendence, more properly has taken the form of a vertical movement, at first foreshadowed by a nostalgia for the future, and now, at the very end of that journey, we discover that it is experienced as a nostalgia for the eternal now of Paradise, embodied in the figure of the sigh, which is transformed into the pilgrim spirit. As a more fitting commentary to this attempt to fathom Dante's ascension of his sigh or pilgrim spirit to behold lady Beatrice, I turn again to *Four Quartets* ("The Dry Salvages") by T.S. Eliot:

> Man's curiosity searches past and future
> And clings to that dimension. But to apprehend
> The point of intersection of the timeless
> With time, is an occupation for the saint—
> No occupation either, but something given
> And taken, in a lifetime's death in love,
> Ardour and selflessness and self-surrender.
> For most of us, there is only the unattended
> Moment, the moment in and out of time,
> The distraction fit, lost in a shaft of sunlight,
> The wild thyme unseen, or the winter lightning
> . . .
> These are only hints and guesses,

Hints followed by guesses; and the rest
Is prayer, observance, discipline, thought and action.
The hint half guessed, the gift half understood, is
    Incarnation.
Here the impossible union
Of spheres of existence is actual,
Here the past and future
Are conquered and reconciled . . .

II

As we now turn our attention to a few examples of the
figure of the sigh in *The Divine Comedy*, I should point out
that the *New Life* ends with words, immediately following
the sonnet *Oltre la spera*, that speak of a "wonderful vision"
that Dante had, which made him "resolve to write no more
of the blessed one . . . until he could more worthily treat of
her." Thus, as it is generally interpreted, the *New Life* ends
by pointing to the future and beyond. Thus its end is a
beginning. We should in fact recall that the title of the "little
book" which, as Dante tells at the beginning of *New Life*, he
is about to copy from his "Book of Memory," bears the
Latin title, *Incipit Vita Nova* (The New Life Begins).

After passing through the Gate of Hell, accompanied
by his guide, Virgil, Dante the pilgrim, is oppressed by
horror as he hears these infernal sounds:

> Quivi sospiri, pianti e alti guai
> risonavan per l'aere sanza stelle.
> perch'io al cominciar ne lagrimai.
>   Diverse lingue, orribili favelle,
> parole di dolore, accenti d'ira,
> voci alte e fioche, e suon di man con elle
>   facevano un tumulto, il qual s'aggira
> sempre in quell'aura sanza tempo tinta,
> come la rena quando turbo spira.
>   (*Inf.* III.22-30)

> Here sighs and lamentations and loud cries,
> were echoing across the starless air,

so that, as soon as I sat out, I wept.
Strange utterances, horrible pronouncements,
accents of anger, words of suffering,
and voices shrill and faint, and beating hands—
all went to make a tumult that will whirl
forever through that turbid, timeless air,
like sand that eddies when a whirlwind swirls.

As we enter this scene, along with Dante the wayfarer and his guide Virgil, we are first struck by the fact that the first sound rising from Hell is that of sighs, thus confirming what we have already attributed to the sigh, that it is a universal, elementary sound that, beyond language, words, may express a number of even conflicting emotions—from anguish to longing, from fear to hope. Here, clearly, sighs are associated with the general cacophony created by the myriad of discordant sounds and voices coming from the damned, which speak of the negation of reason, of harmony, and of the good and the beautiful. However, I would like to state at the outset that the fundamental idea underlying Dante the poet's representation of the state of the damned and the various degrees of their suffering, proportionate to the degree of their negation of the good through their sin, having died unrepentant until the last instant of their life, that such suffering, expressed, for example, by their sighs, reflects their still "saying no to good," in opposition to their natural, absolute will that, by nature, having been created in God's image—as Dante read in Genesis—they still possess. In other words, the unresolved conflict between their relative will to oppose or deny good and their natural, absolute will to choose good constitute essentially their state of damnation and corresponding degree of suffering. Their sighs, therefore, may express a degree of the movement of their absolute will of the good, while at the same time their relative will is bent on denying it. In the words of Étienne Gilson, extracted from his *The Spirit of Medieval Philosophy*, "Since evil is but the corruption of a good and cannot possibly subsist at all save in this good, it follows that inasmuch as there is evil, there is also good. Certainly, we have traveled very far from the degree of order, beauty and measure which God bestowed on the world in creating it, but if sin had abolished all good it would have abolished all being along with the good and the world would no longer exist. In this sense we may say that evil could not eliminate nature without eliminating itself; since it would have no subject left to inhere in, there would be none of which it could be affirmed."[4]

Let us now enter the world of those who loved mere appearances—the lustful—among whom Dante and Virgil encounter Paolo and Francesca, paying special attention to the meaning of the reference made by Dante the wayfarer to the "sweet sighs" experienced by the two lovers before crossing the threshold separating a time of innocence from the time of sinning. Let us first read the question addressed by Dante to Francesca:

> "Ma dimmi: al tempo d'i' dolci sospiri,
> a che e come concedette amore
> che conosceste i dubbiosi disiri?"
> <div align="right">(<i>Inf.</i> V.118-120)</div>

> "But tell me, in the time of the sweet sighs,
> with what and in what way did Love allow you
> to know the dubious desires?"

The opposition between the "sweet sighs" (of longing for what? we may ask), evoking a time of innocence, and the "dubious desires" is clear. Yet, in order to gain a deeper understanding of this conflict, we must interpret at least a measure of the larger context within which we find it formulated by Dante's question. Here is the scene in which Francesca introduces herself to Dante the wayfarer:

> "Siede la terra dove nata fui
> su la marina dove 'l Po discende
> per aver pace co' seguaci sui.

---

[4] Étienne Gilson, *The Spirit of Medieval Philosophy* (New York: Scribner's, 1940), 122.

> Amor, ch'al cor gentil ratto s'apprende,
> prese costui de la bella persona
> che mi fu tolta; e 'l modo ancor m'offende.
>   Amor, ch'a nullo amato amar perdona,
> Mi prese del costui piacer sì forte,
> che, come vedi, ancor non m'abbandona.
>   Amor condusse noi ad una morte.
> Caina attende chi a vita ci spense.
>
> (Inf. V.97-107)

> "The city where I was born lies on that shore
> to which the Po together with the waters
> that follow it descends to be at peace with them.
>   Love that can quickly seize the gentle heart,
> took hold of him because of the fair body
> taken from me—how that was done still wounds me.
>   Love, that releases no beloved from loving,
> took hold of me so strongly through his beauty
> that, as you see, it has not left me yet.
>   Love led the two of us unto one death.
> Caina waits for him who took our life."

The peaceful landscape of Francesca's birthplace (the city of Ravenna, on the Adriatic), which she evokes as a way of introducing herself, stands in sharp contrast to the story of her turbulent, destructive love that immediately (and abruptly) follows. As she depicts her native land, the emphasis falls on the principle of order that governs the power of nature represented by the Po river and its tributaries moving, together, towards their final goal, the sea. The image of the Po that descends to be at peace with its followers calls to mind this passage from Augustine's *Confessions* (XIII.9):

> In thy gift we rest: then we enjoy thee. Our rest is thy gift, our life's place. Love lifts us up thither, and thy good spirit advances our loveliness from the gates of death. In thy good pleasure lies our peace. Our body with is lumpishness strives towards its own place. Weight makes not

downward only, but to its own place also. The fire mounts upward, a stone sinks downward. All things pressed by their own weight go towards their proper places. They are driven by their own weight to seek their own places. Things a little out of their place become unquiet, put them in their order again, and they are quieted. My weight is my love: by that am I carried whithersoever I be carried.

Francesca's landscape symbolizes the natural love which moves all living creatures towards their proper end, God. As the image of the Po seeking peace with its tributaries suggests, to rest in God, or to be His friends, necessarily implies a communion or friendship with others, for the very nature of Divine Love is to gather all loves in its Infinity. With the irruption of the word "Love," uttered by Francesca three times, this landscape and the paradisiacal scene of innocence and harmony that it conjures up prove to be very fragile, just a fleeting recollection of and nostalgia for a lost order and peace. As Roger Dragonetti has observed, "The three tercets [beginning with the word "Amor"] stand out against the background of remembrance of the native land which is the very image of the lost paradise,"[5] which, we may add, is analogous to the "sweet sighs" experienced by the two lovers before their loss of innocence marked by their "dubious desires." The two lovers' natural longing to be, like the Po, united with others within that which transcends them, cannot be fulfilled as long as it is directed to an inappropriate object, a false image of good. Their torment and their hell is caused by the disproportion between the naturally expansive love that can find peace only in Infinite Love—as love of the *Summum Bonum*—and their search for the Infinite in a fleeting image, like that of Francesca's

---

[5] Roger Dragonetti, "L'épisode de Francesca dans le cadre de la convention courtoise," in *Aux frontières du langage poétque: Etudes sur Dante, Mallarmé, Valéry* (Gent: Romanica Gandensia, 1971), 94.

"fair body" and Paolo's "beauty." As Simone Weil has remarked, "Love needs reality. What is more terrible than the discovery that through a bodily appearance we have been loving an imaginary being? It is much more terrible than death, for death does not prevent the beloved from having lived."[6]

III

I will now comment on the figure of the sigh that we find in the scene of Dante's invocation to the constellation Gemini, or the Twins, under which he was born, in the Eighth Heaven, the Sphere of the Fixed Stars, in Canto XXII of *Paradiso*:

> "O gloriose stelle, o lume pregno
> di gran virtù, dal quale io riconosco
> tutto, qual che si sia, il mio ingegno,
>   con voi nasceva e s'ascondeva vosco
> quelli ch'è padre d'ogne mortal vita,
> quand'io senti' di prima l'aere tosco;
>   e poi, quando mi fu grazia largita
> d'entrar ne l'alta rota che vi gira,
> la vostra region mi fu sortita.
>   A voi divotamente ora sospira
> l'anima mia, per acquistar virtute
> al passo forte che a sé la tira.
>   "Tu se' sì presso a l'ultima salute,"
> cominciò Beatrice, "che tu dei
> aver le luci tue chiare e acute;
>   e però, prima che tu t'inlei,
> rimira giù, e vedi quanto mondo
> sotto li piedi già esser ti fei . . . "
>   (*Par.* XXII.112-129)

> O stars of glory, constellation steeped
> in mighty force, all of my genius—

---

[6] *The Simone Weil Reader*, ed. George A. Panichas (New York: McKay, 1977), 359.

whatever be its worth—has you as source:
    with you was born and under you was hidden
he who is father of all mortal lives,
when I first felt the air of Tuscany;
    and then, when grace was granted me to enter
the high wheel that impels your revolutions,
your region was my fated point of entry.
    To you my soul now sighs devotedly,
that it may gain the force for this attempt,
hard trial now demands its every strength.
    "You are so near the final blessedness,"
so Beatrice began, "that you have need
of vision clear and keen; and thus, before
    you enter farther, do look downward, see
what I have set beneath your feet already:
much of the world is there . . . "

The comment that comes to mind is that Dante's sigh here comes at the intersection of two perspectives: of his home in Tuscany and of the present celestial home. This natural, creative connection between the two, in light of the influence on the world below by the "glorious stars," especially their influence on Dante's genius, reminds us of the motif of the pilgrim that we have encountered in the *New Life*, recalling that the pilgrim longs for, sighs for the home he has left behind while longing and sighing for the spiritual, celestial home. Against the backdrop evoked by these observations and recollections, we can now better understand why Dante's invocation or prayer addressed to the "glorious stars" of the constellation of Gemini, is expressed by the devout sighing of his soul, and not, as we read in the *New Life*, especially in the last sonnet, *Oltre la spera (Beyond the sphere)*, by the sighing of his heart, the "new intelligence" placed in it by Love, and, finally, by the "pilgrim spirit." Now that Dante is "near the final blessedness," as Beatrice points out to him, now that he is, finally, in his celestial, spiritual home, it seems appropriate that his prayer expressed by his sigh—to be granted the new power, or "virtute", as a poet, to continue to give form to his vision of Paradise, that still lies ahead, which will end with his vision of God, and as a pilgrim—it seems appropriate, I repeat, that his sigh should now spring from his soul, the spiritual, immortal essence of his being, which at once contains and transcends the "heart," the "new intelligence," and the "pilgrim spirit." The sigh of Dante's soul marks, therefore, the *epiphany* of its "return" to, and *as*, the arch-creative sigh of God, announced by Nicola in his introductory remarks.

I would like to close with these words by T.S. Eliot, from the last of his *Four Quartets* ("Little Gidding"), noting that this poet, who was profoundly influenced by Dante's poetry, here, instead of the common verb "to sigh," uses the verb "suspire," which echoes the Italian verb "sospirare," from "suspirare" in Latin:

> Who then devised the torment? Love.
> Love is the unfamiliar Name
> Behind the bands that wove
> The intolerable shirt of flame
> Which human power cannot remove.
> We only live, only suspire
> Consumed by either fire or fire.

SIGH

Peter Booth

What I am going to present are Hafiz's conceptions of the nature of God, how and why God brought about creation, and man's ultimate state after passing through it. I do not believe it is possible to give a decent reading of Hafiz without these preliminaries, or, to put it another way, I believe so many find Hafiz difficult to read and indeed usually misread him, because they have not read him closely enough to understand these broad contexts. Our entree into this discussion, in keeping with the topic of tonight's presentation, will be Hafiz's use of the word "sigh" as it appears in two couplets. Obviously the reading I will be giving is my own, but as you will see I ground everything by quoting extensively from Hafiz's poetry:

يارب آيينةٌ حسن تو چه جوهر دارد
كه درو آه مرا قوت تأثير نبود[1]

God, what is
the composition of
the mirror
of your beauty
that my sighs
do not have
the power

---

[1] All Persian text is from: حـا فـظ بـر ا سـا س نـسخه نـو يافته بسير كهن [The Divan of Hafiz (Based on a newly discovered manuscript written around the time of Hafiz)], ed. Sayyed Sadeq Sajjadi and Ali Bahramiyan, with notes and commentary by Kazem Bargnaysi (Tehran: Fekr-e-ruz, 2001).

to leave
any trace
on it?

And:

تیر آه ما ز گردون بگذرد حافظ خموش
رحم کن بر جان خود پرهیز کن از تیر ما

The arrow of
our sighs
has shot beyond
the revolutions
of the firmament and fate—
Hafiz, be silent,
have compassion
for your soul
and protect yourself
from our arrow.

Although short and concise, these two couplets and the use
of "sigh" in them carry a wealth of mystical meaning.
Obviously, as I mentioned, to make any headway at all,
Hafiz's use of the word "sigh" will have to be read in the
poetic context establishing the meanings he gives to it. This
is quite an undertaking, as we will have to look at poetic
concepts and a poetic style rarely if ever encountered.
Moreover, the meanings that Hafiz ascribes to "sigh" in
these two couplets are contrary to one another. So let's have
a look at this poetic context. We will start with Hafiz's
broadest concepts and then narrow down to the specific.
But, before beginning, it will be not the least bit helpful to
read a couplet assuring us of failure:

قیاس کردم و تدبیر عقل در ره عشق
چو شبنمی ست که بر بحر میکشد رقمی

I've measured it
and the impression

of reason on
love's path is
like a drop
of dew
drawing a
figure on
the ocean.

With Hafiz's poetry synonymous with or similar to the
path of love, we of course are the ones using reason. Bearing
this in mind, let's start. First, to establish the broad context,
there is no better place to begin than a writer's conception
of creation. In Hafiz, one of these conceptions is in line with
the basic tenets of Islamic mysticism, this being that God,
with the help of angels, formed man out of dust and wine:

دوش دیدم که ملایک در میخانه زدند

گل آدم بسرشتند و به پیمانه زدند

Last night
in the effulgence
of pre-eternity I
saw angels
knocking on
the door of
the tavern
inside they
were kneading
clay with the
wine of
God's love
and casting it
into
the form
of man.[2]

---

[2] This is one of Hafiz's richest and most meaningful couplets.
First, to the Persian mystic, دوش (*dush*) "last night" refers to a
timeless moment in pre-eternity when God sealed the covenant
of love and trust with man by asking him, "Am I not your Lord?"

to which Adam responded "Yes." دوش (*dush*) is frequently associated with powerful, resplendent visions of God interacting with man during the process of man's creation. That is, creation is always happening without a beginning or end. Accordingly, I have translated *dush* to reflect this. Additionally, the Persian word پیمانه (*peymane*) with the auxiliary verb زدن (*zadan*) means "to measure." Its root is پیمان (*peyman*) meaning covenant, treaty, or pact. This again alludes to the original covenant between God and man. پیمانه (*peymane*) also means wine goblet or chalice. پیمانه زدن (*peymane zadan*) means both to "throw" a pot, cup or chalice (in the pottery sense), as well as to quaff a gulp of wine. Taking all of this together we can glimpse, even in translation, Hafiz's poetic genius. Taverns, Zoroastrian taverns, were dilapidated structures of gambling, prostitution, and alcohol located on the edge of cities. In Islamic times they were tolerated as they provided substantial tax revenues. In Hafiz's poetry, they become a symbol for the ruined state of man after his "fall" from paradise. Hafiz also uses them to show that the grace and existence of God is limitless and can appear anywhere, as well as to express that God is not a moralist and that no one is condemned, or excluded from His Love. In a higher sense, and one well established in Persian mystical poetry before Hafiz through the poetry of Sinai, Attar and Rumi, the tavern is a metaphorical spiritual state where man's lower self is annihilated (فنا / *fana*) so that his true existence as God can manifest. Hafiz extends this meaning to include the destruction of the foundation of one spiritual state so that he can move onto the next higher spiritual state. In Hafiz's cosmology then, the tavern is where spiritual advancement takes places through the ruin of one spiritual state brought about by the intoxication of God's love (wine). These assertions are well supported by this couplet:

بر در میخانهٔ عشق ای ملک تسبیح گوی
کندر آنجا طینت آدم مخمّر میکنند

Angel, sing praises at the door of the wine tavern of love
for inside they are kneading into form the nature of man.

The Persian mystics believed that every particle of man was composed of dust and the wine of God's love carefully kneaded by the angels under God's instructions into human form over a forty-day period. This process expresses the descent of man's

In this description, there is a mixing of a divine existence with a substance that is material and separate from this divine existence. Hafiz upholds that this mixing is just that.[3] God's eternal existence is never changed, impressioned or altered in any way by His creation of creation and mankind. That is, to use a scientific term, creation is just a mixture, a compound is never formed. Both the wine representing God's existence and the clay representing material creation ultimately precipitate out from one another, just as sand precipitates out from turbid water, leaving God's essential, uncreated nature unaltered in any way by His creation of the universe and humanity.

As we read further, we encounter Hafiz's assertion that creation, rather than being something, is absolutely nothing, this nothing of creation having been created out of the everything of God. And this nothing, as Hafiz expresses over and over again, is absolutely nothing. It is not dust compounded with the wine of God's essence to form another lasting existence. It is just nothing:

حاصل کارگه کون و مکان این همه نیست
باده پیش ار که اسباب جهان این همه نیست

The total
production of

---

spirit into human form. It is the undoing of this process, expressed in Hafiz's poetry, that is the ascension of man's soul back to its source with God. The Persian mystics term the culmination of this process as وصل خدا (*vasle khoda*) "union with God" or God-Realization. They termed this unfoldment راة خدا (*rahe khoda*) "the spiritual path." This is the subject of Hafiz's poetry. For a more detailed discussion, see Annemarie Schimmel, *A Two-Colored Brocade: The Imagery of Persian Poetry* (Chapel Hill: University of North Carolina Press, 1992), 57-60 and Agu Ashgar Syed-Gohrab, "The Erotic Spirit," in *Hafiz and the Religion of Love in Classical Persian Poetry*, ed. Leonard Lewisohn (London: I.B. Tauris, 2010), 116.

[3] For a more detailed discussion, see Lewisohn, *Hafiz and the Religion of Love*, 116-7.

the created
universe is
absolutely
nothing
bring wine
for everything
in the
material world
does not
exist.

This complete separation of the two—God from His creation—is one of the basic themes of Hafiz's poetry. And, as Hafiz sees it, the two are always totally separate by virtue of one fact—the nothing of creation is relative as it has a point of origin making everything within it relative whereas, without a point of origin, *there is no relativity in the uncreated existence of God.* Moreover, there can be no relationship between the two as lacking a point of origin there is no benchmark within God for everything created and possessing the relative benchmark of origin to connect with. Expressed another way, the two are like oil and water, as in God's non-relative being there is no interface for the relativity of creation to adhere to. In the poetic expression of this relationship, Hafiz encounters the same difficulty every presenter of the concepts of God's infinity and the process of His creation encounters—how to make the infinite, uncreated existence of God and the process of the creation of the nothing of the universe tangible to the created, limited, relative, rational mind of man. Rather than revert to myth, as most do, Hafiz writes from his own conception of the relationship—or actually the lack of it. In so doing, he makes this distinction the scaffolding for his poetic expression.

Obviously, as the relative, rational mind and reason have no ability to fully conceive of the non-relative infinite existence of God, the best Hafiz can do is to qualify it, using the tools of metaphor and simile that poets are required to use. As he says:

ز وصف حسن تو حافظ چگونه نطق زند
که چون صفات الهی ورای ادراکی

How can
Hafiz use
words to
describe
your beauty
when the
qualities of
God are
outside
the perceptions
of man?

When writing about the God that Hafiz perceives, this is difficult as being non-relative there is no measure, dimension or time in God's uncreated existence, making this existence inconceivable to a form of perception born in time and space—the relative, rational mind. Nonetheless, Hafiz attempts to do this in many different ways, but behind all of his writing is the presentation of God's absolute independence of everything in creation, as this is His state. This is qualified, as it must be, in numerous ingenious ways:

گریهٔ حافظ چه سنجد پیش استغنای عشق
کندرین طوفان نماید هفت دریا شبنمی

What measure
do Hafiz's
tears have
before the
independence
of love
when in
this typhoon
the seven seas
appear as

a drop
of dew?

Or:

به هوش باش که هنگام باد استغنا
هزار خرمن طاعت به نیم جو ننهند

Be careful
for when the
wind of
God's absolute
independent nature
blows
a thousand
harvests of
obedience will
not be worth
half a grain
of barley.

Or:

اسمان گو مفروش این عظمت کندر عشق
خرمن مه به جوی خوشهٔ پروین به دو جو

Tell the sky
not to show off
its immensity
for in love
the harvest
of the moon
is not worth
a grain of
barley and
the cluster of
Pleiades
is not worth
two.

Returning now to the first of our two couplets containing "sigh," and bearing in mind that Hafiz is using the tangible, or created, to allude to and give a sense of the intangible, or uncreated—that is God as infinite love—while also establishing that the two remain completely separate from one another—we find that his use of "sigh" and "mirror" in the first couplet is a perfect illustration of this broad poetic context. Let's read the first couplet again:

یارب آیینهٔ حسن تو چه جوهر دارد
که درو آه مرا قدرت تأثیر نبود

God, what is
the composition of
the mirror
of your beauty
that my sighs
do not have
the power
to leave
any trace
on it?

Although the lover, through his sighs, is trying to impress the Beloved, this is ultimately impossible as the Beloved, being uncreated, lacks the relativity necessary for the relative sighs of the created lover to interface with. "The composition of the mirror of your beauty" is then a symbol for the non-relative uncreated existence of God and this is why "my sighs" being created or relative, "do not have the power to leave any trace on it." The articulation of this metaphoric construct is commonly encountered in Hafiz. Indeed, again, it is the very scaffolding of his presentation of the interaction between God as the Beloved and His created lover.

Our reading of this first couplet provides a good introduction to the second, which is far more complex and dynamic than the first. In this second couplet, "sigh" is used to express God's being as limitless, uncreated Love. In the first couplet, it was "the mirror of your beauty" that did this, with sigh being the opposite of this mirror as it represented the created and limited. Considering this "pivoting of imagery" we find that Hafiz will use the same object to mean totally opposite things with the "pivot" of meaning turning between the opposite poles of the limitless uncreated nature of God as one boundless extreme and the limited nature of his creation and His created lover as the other. As Hafiz sees it, this curving, turning or pivoting is necessary for the illusion of creation to come into existence, and his expressing this throughout his poetic imagery is not done to draw the reader more deeply into illusion so much as it is to draw him out of it. Be that as it may, returning to our couplet, there are phrases and symbols that, to the one who has taken the time to read Hafiz closely, make this representative use of "sigh" very clear. Let's read the couplet again:

تیر آه ما ز گردون بگذرد حافظ خموش
رحم کن بر جان خود پرهیز کن از تیر ما

The arrow of
our sighs
has shot beyond
the revolutions
of the firmament and fate—
Hafiz, be silent,
have compassion
for your soul
and protect yourself
from our arrow.

This expression of an uncreated Love outside of time and space is commonly encountered in Hafiz with different symbols representing it. These reinforce our uncreated/created, non-relative/relative reading:

گوهری کز صدف کون و مکان بیرون است
طلب از گمشدگان رو دریا میکرد

43

My heart
sought from
those lost
along the shore
the pearl outside
of the shell of
the created
universe of
time and
space.

("The pearl" here is one of the symbols for God-realization
in Hafiz.)

Returning to the first couplet, it is very rare for Hafiz
(unlike Rumi) to tell himself to be quiet. On the contrary,
Hafiz views himself as the one who should speak as is seen
here:

سخن اندر دهان دوست گوهر
ولیکن گفتهء حافظ از آن به

Words in the
Beloved's mouth
are like pearls
but Hafiz's speech
is better.

An expression further illumined by this couplet:

راست چون سوسن و گل از اثر صحبت پاک
در زبان بود مرا هرچه تو را در دل بود

I as the
white lily
and you Beloved
as the
red rose
we were in
pure companionship
and whatever was

in your heart
was spoken by
my tongue.[4]

In Persian poetry, the lily represents the tongue of speech
as its petals are shaped like the tongue. The red rose,
representing the Beloved, does not have petals whose shape
allows it to speak. Hence, the white lily, here representing
the tongue of the lover, speaks whatever is in the heart of
the red rose representing the Beloved. Or, to put it another
way, it is the nightingale, representing the lover, who,
inspired by the Beloved, represented by the red rose, sings
to the Beloved, and not the other way around. Nonetheless,
it is the Rose, or Beloved, who teaches the lily, or lover, the
subtleties of speech:

مرا تا عشق تعلیم سخن کرد
بود هر محفلی نکتّه حدیثم

From the time
He taught me the
words of love
my sayings as
subtleties are
discussed in
every circle.

So, for Hafiz to tell himself to be silent establishes "the
arrow of our sighs" as a superlative as it is in a realm beyond
the incomparable role Hafiz establishes for himself as the
tongue revealing God's most intimate nature.[5] Reading
further we find that "the arrow" carries with it a wealth of
contextually established images, the most primary of these
being that Hafiz presents the Beloved—God—as being
perfectly straight or erect—here like an arrow—while all

---

[4] For a discussion of the imagery of the lily, see Schimmel, *A Two-Colored Brocade*, 166.
[5] Hafiz's appellation is *lisan al-ghayb*, "the tongue of the hidden mysteries."

else in the illusion of His creation is presented with some degree of curvature. That is simply put, as Hafiz presents it, for anything to appear to exist it must be curved.

Just as in the beginning we encountered wine as representing the uncreated existence of God as Infinite Love, with dust or clay representing His creation, so too here we have erectness and straightness representing God's uncreated, unmanifest state, with curvature, and all that is curved, representing His creation. Returning to our straight arrow, we find that we are only scratching the surface as, obviously, this arrow is a weapon of violent aggression. Let's read our couplet again:

تیر آه ما ز گردون بگذرد حافظ خموش
رحم کن بر جان خود پرهیز کن از تیر ما

> The arrow of
> our sighs
> has shot beyond
> the revolutions
> of the firmament and fate—
> Hafiz, be silent,
> have compassion
> for your soul
> and protect yourself
> from our arrow.

Again, the arrow represents a violently aggressive manifestation of God's Love. Moreover, reading in context, we find that man's love for God, born as it is in the darkness and illusion of separation, can become so great that even God becomes jealous of it. This great love of man for God in Hafiz is then referred to as "the treasure" and this treasure is attacked or plundered by God, represented here as an arrow, but elsewhere also as a blood-thirsty Turkish warlord:

خیز تا خاطر بدان ترک سمرقندی دهیم
کز لبانش بوی خون عاشقان آید همی

46

Raise and
give our
hearts to
that Turk
from
Samarkhand
for from
His lips is
the fragrance
of the blood
of His lovers.

Or:

از چشم شوخش ای دل ایمان خود نگه دار
کان جادوی کمان کش بر عزم غارت آمد

Heart
protect your faith
from His
saucy eyes
for that Magician
with a bow
has come
to plunder.

In short, God, unable to stand His own separation
from the intensity of the love of His lover, launches nothing
less than a full-throttled assault on His lover's heart. Each
of these attacks brings the victim closer and closer to Union
with God. Again, our couplet:

تیر آه ما ز گردون بگذرد حافظ خموش
رحم کن بر جان خود پرهیز کن از تیر ما

The arrow of
our sighs
has shot beyond
the revolutions
of the firmament and fate—

> Hafiz, be silent,
> have compassion
> for your soul
> and protect yourself
> from our arrow.

Given that this description is voiced by a group, "our" adds another dynamic to our reading. Since the arrow has shot beyond the revolutions of the universe, the ones claiming it as "our arrow" can be none other than God-realized souls as they have gone outside the limits of creation. This state of these souls as God-realized is not just established by the context of this couplet, but also by Hafiz's larger context, as anyone who has gone outside the bounds of creation has become united with God. The purpose and final goal of existence permeate Hafiz's imagery and that is what we see here. Considering this we now have to relate the first line of the couplet to the second line, "Hafiz, be silent, have compassion for your soul and protect yourself from our arrow." Again, within the context of Hafiz's imagery, the arrow means only one thing—the metaphoric representation of the violent manifestation of God's Love. Returning for a moment to the larger picture, as God's existence as infinite Love is uncreated and non-relative, it not only does not have any measure in it, but also does not have any volume as volume is nothing more than a relative measure. Put simply, this means that although God is the only existence, His existence has no volume or substance. And quite obviously, if something has no substance, it is impossible for something with substance—be it an illusory substance—to find a foundation or footing in it. Once again, the non-relative and the relative cannot interface with one another. That is to say, the foundation of the separateness of the lover is not built on God but entwined and built on the lover himself. As the violent manifestation of the arrow of God's love has no substance, it uproots the foundation or "substance" of the lover's separateness when it strikes, and, as Hafiz presents it, this uprooting, even though it brings the lover closer to the Beloved, is very painful and shattering. It is for this reason that Hafiz is told to protect himself from the arrow of the sigh of the God-realized, as the wound from this arrow uproots the very foundation of the ego and separate existence. This "uprooting" occasioned by the manifestation of God's presence is at the core of spiritual advancement in Hafiz's poetry. Consider these couplets:

اساس توبه که در محکمی چو سنگ نمود
ببین که جام زجاجی چه طرفه اش بشکست

See how the
foundations
of repentance
that appear
in strength
as a rock
are shattered
by a crystal goblet
of wine.

Or:

حالیا عشوهٔ عشق تو ز بنیادم برد
تا دگر باره حکیمانه چه بنیاد کند

Now the
coquettishness
of your love
has uprooted
my foundation
until again
it will wisely
lay another.

Or:

بیا که قصر امل سخت سست بنیاد ست
بیار باده که بنیاد عمر بر باد ست

49

Come, for the
foundations of
the palace of
desire are
very weak;
bring wine
for the
footings of
life are on
the wind.

Or:

اگرچه مستی عشقم خراب کرد ولی
اساس هستی من زان خراب آبادست

Although
the intoxication
of love
ruined me
the foundation
of my existence
in that ruin
flourishes.[6]

So, ultimately, whether our entree is through a "sigh"
or any of the other vast array of metaphors on Hafiz's
palette, we arrive at his artistic intention, and this is to write
the poetry of God-realization:

---

[6] This couplet may refer to verse 72 in the Koran. It is a concise
description of the process of progression on the spiritual path
where one state or stage is uprooted to be replaced by the
foundation of a higher state or stage that, in turn, is then
uprooted as the lover of God progresses towards union with his
Beloved. See Hossein-Ali Heravi, *A Commentary on the Ghazals
of Hafiz* (Nashre Now Publishing Company, 1988), I.229.

ز مهربان سرا پرادهٔ وصال شوم
ز بندگان خداوندگار خود باشم

I have
become
one of the
inhabitants
of the
realm of
Union
may it be
that I
remain the
slave
of my
Beloved God.

Or:

این سرکشی کنگرهٔ کاخ وصل راست
سرها بر آستانهٔ او خاک در شود

The elevation of
the ramparts of
the palace of union
is so high that
innumerable heads
have become
dust on the
threshold of
its door.

Or:

حافظ شکایت از غم هجران چه میکنی
در هجر وصل باشد و در ظلمت است نور

Hafiz
why do

you complain
about the
sorrow
of separation
in separation
there is
union
and in
darkness
light.

Or:

حافظ شاید اگر در طلب گوهر وصل
دیده دریا کنم از اشک و در و غوطه خورم

Hafiz
perhaps in
pursuit of
the pearl
of Union
you can
form an
ocean from
your tears
and drown
in it.[7]

---

[7] The use of "pearl" here recalls and defines the use of "pearl" in the couplet quoted at the beginning:

گوهری کز صدف کون و مکون بیرون است
طلب از گمشداگان ره دریا میکرد

My heart
sought from
those lost
along the shore
the pearl outside
of the shell of
the created

Or:

زاد راه حرم وصل نداریم مگر
به گدایی ز در میکده زادی طلبیم

We do not
have the
provisions
necessary
to traverse
the path to
the sanctuary
of Union
unless
we beg
for them
in poverty
at the door
of the
tavern.

Or:

غرض ز مسجد و میخانه ام وصال شماست
جز این خیال ندارم خدا گواه من است

My intention
in both
the mosque
and the
tavern is
union with
you aside
from
this I have

---

universe of
time and
space.

no other
thought as
God is
my witness.

Or finally:

شکر خدا که هرچه طلب کردم از خدا

بر منتهای همت خود کامران شدم

Thanks to God
that whatever
I sought
from Him
to the limits
of my ambition
I gained.

Now, returning again to our second couplet, as I
mentioned, the phrase "our arrow" suggests a group of
souls who have completed the spiritual journey and
obtained the Union with God that Hafiz speaks of in the
above couplets. Once again, considering for a moment the
broad context, in Islamic mysticism (as well as Hafiz) this
union is achieved through the annihilation—فنا (*fana*)—
and not the preservation of the limited, individual self.[8]
Yet, these souls ("our") are speaking to Hafiz after this
annihilation. That is, although united with God after
having been annihilated, they are speaking as individual
personalities. This would seem to be impossible, and yet,
throughout Hafiz, we encounter personalities who express
individuality after the annihilation that results in God-
realization. We will not have done justice to our brief visit
to this great poet if we do not take a deeper look at this

---

[8] *Fana-baqa*, see Schimmel, *Mystical Dimensions of Islam* (Chapel
Hill: University of North Carolina Press, 1975), 222 and
Lewisohn, *Hafiz and the Religion of Love*, 113, for a discussion of
the history of annihilation in Islamic mystics.

dilemma, and this is where another facet of this genius lies, as he has, I believe, through experience, figured out the physics of existence. Simply, in Hafiz the annihilation is the annihilation of the relativity and curving that brings creation and the lover into existence; it is not the annihilation of the lover's individuality that his passing through this "curvature" or creation creates. Consider for a moment if this were not the case, if Love created separation to put the lover through all of the painful situations that the experience of love in illusion entails, just in the end to completely annihilate the lover's existence with only the original infinity of God remaining. That wouldn't be love so much as it would be mindless torture. In Hafiz then, infinite individuality is maintained after annihilation, as the annihilation is just the annihilation of substance, volume and any relativity. Now, finally, for those of you who think about it, it is assumed that for individuality within union with God to be achieved, the united, individual lover must be in "lock step" with God, part of a "body politic" as it were. However, if this were the condition of the lover's union with God then God's infinite love would become conditional. This also is not possible for a conditioned love loses its infinity, and in losing its infinity love is no longer love. In short, the highest expression of love—the only possible expression of love as found in Hafiz's poetry—is for love to create another perfect in its composition, without any bounds or conditions, infinite and completely, eternally, free.

Having attempted to achieve the impossible, let's return to a measure of our failure. As Hafiz says:

میان او که خدا آفریده است از هیچ
دقیقه ی ست که هیچ آفریده نگشاده ست

Her waist
that God
created out
of nothing
is so slender

none created
can embrace it

Or:

نهادم عقل را ره توشه از می
ز شهر هستی اش کردم روانه

I gave
reason
wine
as a
provision
for the
road
and sent
him
out of
the city
of existence.

Or:

قیاس کردم و تدبیر عقل در ره عشق
چو شبنمی ست که بر بحر میکشد رقمی

I have
measured it
and the impression
of reason on
love's path
is like a
drop of dew
drawing a figure
on the ocean.

As these vast concepts permeate all aspects of Hafiz's poetry, we will take a deeper look at his cosmology in the next essay, "Gaze."

ON THE GAZE

Nicola Masciandaro

Who can fix a limit to the gaze? Who will dare to define its scope, point out its center, or draw a circle around its sphere? As far as I can see, everyone turns away. Where? To the gaze.

On the one hand, the gaze is limitless, extending in all directions, further than the eye can see. "The self," says Ibn Arabi, "is an ocean without shore. Gazing upon it has no end in this world and the next."

On the other hand, the gaze is nothing, nothing but itself, a zero through which only another I is looking. "All creatures are absolutely nothing," says Johannes Tauler, "That which has no being is nothing. And creatures have no being, because they have their being in God; if God turned away for a moment, they would cease to exist."

Is my gaze my own? Yes and no. I look, yet cannot see myself. I am seen, yet none sees me. Is that you, looking back at yourself in the mirror? No and yes. The gaze is the mirror of the gaze, every look a reflection of itself. Where would I be, what would become of you—everything—if that which sees and is seen by seeing, vision's own visibility, were blotted out, blinded? If the gaze through which we gaze shut its eyes? "Do not separate from me," says Hafiz, "for you are the light of my vision. / You are the peace of my soul and the intimate of my heart."

I see that one is always turning toward and turning away, turning away from what one turns toward, turning toward

58

what one turns away from. What an endless revolution, the restless conversion of the still, ever-spinning eye. Zoom in on planet pupil, a little nothing meaning all, suspended in its own universal reflection, projecting and filming everything through the point, the navel of itself. Is your gaze born from you or you from your gaze? "I believe," says Dante in *Paradiso*, "because of the sharpness of the living ray that I sustained, that I would have been lost if my eyes had turned away from it."

Admit it, the gaze is really too much. Who can withstand it? *No one shall see me and live.* That must be why Narcissus never stops spontaneously lying to himself about his reflection, never ceases to fall in love with his own image, seeing neither that it is an image nor his. If you are me then who am I? If I am me then who are you? Perpetual predicament of the illusion that sustains reality. As Meher Baba once rhymed, "Oh, you ignorant, all-knowing Soul / what a plight you are in! / Oh, you weak, all-powerful Soul / what a plight you are in! / Oh, you miserable, all-happy Soul / what a plight you are in! / What a plight! / What a sight! / What a delight!"

How eternally precious those passing moments, when the gaze opens itself a little more and sees, by some unfathomable magic or trick of the abyss which if you gaze long into it gazes back into you (N), that the image is no less in love with Narcissus. As Francis Brabazon said, "And so one arrives at the painful conclusion that the Beloved alone exists—which means that oneself doesn't. And that's a terrible predicament to find oneself in—for one is still *there*! The only solution I found was to accept the position: 'You alone are and I am not, but we are both here.'"

Whose gaze is *that*? What eye calmly turns itself towards the gaze of the real, penetrating the sight of life, which is death to the living? It would seem as if the person who possesses this look also cannot sustain it. Are not saints, or the truly beautiful, forever ashamed of their own eyes? Here is a passage from Meher Baba to fall in love with: "A wali . . .

has the power to open the third eye and grant divine sight, if he is in the mood. He can do so by simply looking into the eyes of the aspirant, even if the aspirant is at a distance. When the third eye is opened, all is light . . . It is so powerful an experience that the recipient either goes mad or drops the body . . . One type of wali is called artad. They are very, very few, quite rare. They are very fiery, with piercing eyes that break through anything, even mountains! Their gaze is sufficient to cut an animal in two, hence they always keep their eyes on the ground. That too is split apart."

If the gaze splits, surely that is because it is without number, because the manyness of our eyes only sees by reflecting *one*. Thus the individual neither sees nor is seen by unity without being cut in two. Consider this as the principle of honesty or natural self-discernment. I am only whole, authentic, truthful, when I see how double, how dark to myself I am, when *eye* see myself seen by seeing itself. "Look not upon me, because I am black, because the sun hath looked upon me" (Song of Songs 1:6).

Imagine a map of all vision, a long tracing of its every line, individual and collective, from the beginningless beginning to the endless end, from the earliest emergence of anything to its final absolute evaporation. A one-to-one map scaled to the continuum of seeing itself, all of its sleeps and wakings, every stop and start across the seas of every kingdom of being, in short, from stone to human. What does it look like? In his *Dialogue on the Two Principle Systems of the World*, Galileo, in order to explain how "this motion in common [i.e. the motion of the earth] . . . remains as if nonexistent to everything that participates in it," conceives the figure of an artist who draws, without separating pen and paper, everything he sees while sailing from Italy to Turkey: "if an artist had begun drawing with that pen on a sheet of paper when he left the port and had continued doing so all the way to Alexandretta [*Iskenderun*], he would have been able to derive from the pen's motion a whole narrative of many figures, completely traced and sketched in thousands of directions, with landscapes, buildings, animals, and other things. Yet the actual real essential movement marked by the pen point would have been only a line; long, indeed, but very simple. But as to the artist's own actions, these would have been conducted exactly the same as if the ship had been standing still" (Galileo Galilei). Is not the real hero of the story the hyper-saccadic story of the eye? Now raise that to the power of itself *ad infinitum*. What a line!

More locally, the gaze concerns the duration and depth of seeing, the extensity and intensity of its time and space. Gazing not only looks but looks beyond looking, exploring the very surface of vision as a dimension otherwise than surface. The gaze sees by seeing into seeing itself, in both senses at once. No need for a map, the gaze directs itself. As Merleau-Ponty explains, the focus of the gaze, through which we establish the qualities of objects by interrupting them from "the total life of the spectacle," operates through an essential reflexivity: "The sensible quality, far from being coextensive with perception, is the peculiar product of an attitude of curiosity or observation. It appears when, instead of yielding up the whole of my gaze to the world, I turn toward this gaze itself, and when I ask myself *what precisely it is that I see*; it does not occur in the natural transactions between my sight and the world, it is the reply to a certain kind of questioning on the part of my gaze, the outcome of a second order or critical kind of vision which tries to know itself in its own particularity."

So we are led back, willy nilly, to the essential gravity of the gaze as an exponent of will, to looking as the weight of the love of a being who is its own self-consuming question. But what of the one whose will is annihilated? "To those in whom the will has turned and denied itself," says Schopenhauer, "this very real world of ours, with all its suns and galaxies, is—nothing."

What does the gaze that sees nothing see? "And Saul arose from the earth; and when his eyes were opened, he saw nothing" (Acts 9:8).

I trust that both Dante and Hafiz agree that this gaze sees
not only nothing, but everything. As their contemporary
Meister Eckhart says, "A man who is established thus in
God's will wants nothing but what is God's will and what is
God . . . Even though it meant the pains of hell it would be
joy and happiness to him. He is free and has left self behind,
and must be free of whatever is to come in to him: if my eye
is to perceive color, it must be free of all color. If I see a blue
or white color, the sight of my eye which sees the color, the
very thing that sees, is the same as that which is seen by the
eye. The eye with which I see God is the same eye with
which God sees me: my eye and God's eye are one eye, one
seeing, one knowing and one love."

This makes me want to see what these two poets might see
looking into each other. For both are so well versed in the
mystery of the unitive doubleness of vision experienced in
the gaze, wherein the two-ness of the eyes becomes one. As
Hadewych explains, "The power of sight that is created as
natural to the soul is charity. This power of sight has two
eyes, love and reason. Reason cannot see God except in
what he is not; love rests not except in what he is. Reason
has its secure paths, by which it proceeds. Love experiences
failure, but failure advances it more than reason. Reason
advances toward what God is, by means of what God is not.
Love sets aside what God is not and rejoices that it fails in
what God is. Reason has more satisfaction than love, but
love has more sweetness of bliss than reason. These two,
however, are of great mutual help one to the other; for
reason instructs love, and love enlightens reason. When
reason abandons itself to love's wish, and love consents to
be forced and held within the bounds of reason, they can
accomplish a very great work. This no one can learn except
by experience."

And I am looking forward to this encounter all the more,
not only because, as Vernon Howard says, "Anything you
look forward to will destroy you, as it already has," but
because what is seen between the gazes of these two poets

will no doubt be something neither could see—the beauty of a spark leaping between the eyes of two no-ones.

As Hafiz says, "اهل نظر دو نظر در یک عالم ببازند" [Men of sight can lose both worlds in one glance]. Or as Love tells Dante in the *Vita Nuova*, "Ego tanquam centrum circuli . . . tu autem non sic" [I am as the centre of a circle . . . you however are not so].

Dante's Gaze

Franco Masciandaro

I

Let us turn our attention to some unique moments in the *Vita Nuova* (*The New Life*), the youthful work written by Dante after the death of Beatrice, in 1290, and later in his mature work, and more widely known, *The Divine Comedy*, in which the figure of the gaze stands out as a sign of heightened creativity. The gaze, a secret, ultimately unfathomable language unto itself, like the sigh, the smile, the voice, or tears, is at once *before* and *beyond* language, that is, before and beyond discursive reasoning, like silent prayer.

The second chapter of *The New Life* opens with these words:

> Nine times since my birth had the heaven of light returned to almost the same point in its orbit when to my eyes first appeared the glorious lady of my mind, who was called Beatrice . . . She appeared humbly and properly dressed in a most noble color, crimson, girded and adorned in the manner that befitted her so youthful age. At that moment I say truly that the spirit of life, which dwells in the most secret chamber of the heart, began to tremble so strongly that it appeared terrifying in its smallest veins; and trembling it said these words: "Behold a god more powerful than I, who comes to rule over me." At that point the animal spirit, which dwells in the upper chamber to which all the spirits of the senses

carry their perceptions, began to marvel greatly, and speaking especially to the spirits of sight, it said these words: "Now has appeared your beatitude." . . . Love ruled over my soul . . . Many times he commanded that I seek to behold this youthful angel; thus many times in my childhood I sought her, and I saw in her such noble and laudable bearing that of her could certainly be said those words of the poet Homer: "She seemed no child of mortal man but of god."[15]

As we read this passage, we are struck by the way Dante speaks of the moment he first saw Beatrice—when he was nine and she was nearly nine—as he does not say the he *saw* Beatrice, but that she *appeared to his eyes.* He also speaks of his and her age in astronomical terms, thus emphasizing the objective reality of Beatrice's first appearance to Dante, *before* such experience is internalized and thus it is perceived, not as a mere happening, but as an *event,* that of *his vision* of her, as he will state later, when he describes the inner drama of the "spirit of life" that, "trembling," spoke of the god of Love, and of the "animal spirit" that, marveling greatly, addressed its words *especially to the spirits of sight.* Only after this drama has been played out does Dante, moved by Love to behold Beatrice ("the youthful angel"), state that he *saw* her. We should also note that Dante, as he recalls his first encounter with Beatrice as a child, also speaks of her as "the glorious lady" of his mind, that is, of Beatrice already dead and dwelling in Heaven. Thus, Dante poet and lover, as he introduces the beloved, reveals the intersection of the moment in time, the *then* of her appearance, and the eternal *now* of her dwelling in Paradise.

Hence, as he begins to select and transcribe passages that he reads in his Book of Memory, of which he spoke in the first chapter of *The New Life,* he offers us a foretaste of

---

[15] Dante Alighieri, *Vita Nuova,* trans. Dino S. Cervigni and Edward Vasta (Notre Dame: University of Notre Dame Press, 1995), 47-48.

his poetics of the gaze, which informs many pages of this work.

In Chapter III we find the first example of the creative power of Beatrice's gaze:

> After many days had passed, so that precisely nine years were completed following the appearance described above of this most gentle lady, it happened that on the last of these days this marvelous lady appeared to me dressed in purest white, between two gentle ladies who were of greater years; and passing along a street, she turned her eyes to that place where I stood in great fear, and in her ineffable courtesy, which today is rewarded in life everlasting, she greeted me with exceeding virtue, such that I then seemed to see all the terms of beatitude.

Of special significance in this scene of Dante's encounter with Beatrice, nine years after her first appearance to him as one comparable to a child "not of mortal man, but of god," is that Beatrice's gaze precedes and, in a sense, transcends her greeting directed at Dante. We might say that it is the first, silent expression of her words, *before* these take shape and are manifested. I should also note that here Beatrice's gaze does not meet Dante's gaze, but, as Dante the author notes, *she turned her eyes to that place where [he] stood in great fear.* This suggests that, as the poet and lover *stands in fear* as *he* gazes at the scene of Beatrice appearing in a street of Florence, accompanied by two gentle ladies, is not able to direct his "spirits of sight" towards those of the beloved. Why? I think that he cannot because he *fears* that such an encounter with the inner being manifested through the gaze of such an extraordinary lady, whose greeting seems to confer beatitude to him, would overwhelm him. He could not endure the vision of what Emmanuel Levinas has called "the Infinity of the Other." These words by T. S. Eliot come to mind, from "Burnt Norton," the first of his *Four Quartets*: "Go, go, go, said the bird: human kind / cannot bear very much reality." Indeed! Think for a moment: How long can each one of us here sustain, or endure gazing into each other's eyes before we feel uncomfortable and feel compelled to turn our gaze *away from very much reality— the Infinity of the Other!*

Dante discovers a new way of experiencing the beatitude once conferred to him by his beloved's greeting by singing her praises and directing them not only to Beatrice, but to a larger audience—a community of ladies endowed with a noble heart, a *cor gentil,* beginning with a chorus of those ladies whom he addresses with the words of the famous *canzone, Donne ch'avete intelletto d'amore (Ladies who have understanding of love),* which marks the beginning of a new poetics, the poetics of praise (la poetica della lode). In the following excerpt extracted from this complex, rich *canzone* (Chapter XIX) we shall discover— woven in this new poetics—the poetics of the gaze, and thus a new measure of the larger economy of the salvific power of Beatrice's presence, which transcends the earlier narrow economy whereby her greeting was defined for its power to confer beatitude mainly on Dante:

> The lady is desired in highest heaven:
> now I wish to have you know of her virtue.
> I say, let who wishes to appear a gentle lady
> go with her, for when she goes along the way,
> into villainous hearts Love casts a chill,
> whereby all their thoughts freeze and perish;
> and who might suffer to stay and behold her
> would change into a noble thing, or die.
> And when she finds someone worthy
> to behold her, he experiences her power,
> for what she gives him turns into salvation,
> and so humbles him that he forgets every offense.
> God has given her an even greater grace:
> that one cannot end in evil who has spoken to her.
> Of her says Love: "A mortal thing,
> how can it be so adorned and pure?"
> He then looks at her again, and within himself swears
> that God intends to make of her something new.
> . . .

From her eyes, however she moves them,
issue spirits of love inflamed,
which wound the eyes of whoever then beholds her
and pass through so that each finds the heart;
you see Love depicted in her face,
there where none may behold her steadily.

As we read these verses, we are first struck by the
absence of any reference to Dante the poet and lover's role
as one who beholds Beatrice or is the object of her salvific
gaze. Emphasis instead is given to the following actors in
what can be perceived as a little drama: the first is one who
"might suffer to stay and behold" Beatrice, who "would
change into a noble thing, or die." In light of the principle
of analogy underlying this action, we may think of two
passages from the Book of Exodus: in the first we read that
"Yahweh would speak with Moses face to face, as a man
speaks with his friend" (Exodus 33.11); in the second—
from the same chapter, a few verses below—we read:
"Moses said [to Yahweh], 'Show me your glory, I beg you.'
And he said, 'I will let all my splendor pass in front of you,
and I will pronounce before you the name Yahweh' . . . 'You
cannot see my face,' he said, 'for man cannot see me and
live.'" The second actor is one whom Beatrice deems
"worthy to behold her," and to whom she confers the gift
of salvation, whereby he is so humbled that he "forgets
every offense." The third actor is the god of Love, who,
filled with wonder about Beatrice's miraculous, salvific
power, exclaims: "a mortal thing, / how can it be so
adorned and pure?" Significantly, he then "looks at her
again," and, in a kind of inner dialogue with himself, speaks
of God (with the capitol 'G'), Who "intends to make of
[Beatrice] something new," that is, a miracle. With this
reference to God, Who is Infinite Love, the god of Love
reminds us readers that what we earlier defined as drama in
human terms is in fact a theo-drama, which—we may now
recognize retrospectively—has been announced by these
verses, "the lady is desired in highest heaven." The fourth
character in what we have just defined as a theo-drama is
Beatrice. We now witness at once a phenomenology of the

spirits of sight, which are at once a manifestation of the physical power of sight and of the spiritual, mystical power that speak of them as "spirits of love inflamed." Paradoxically, these spirits, as messengers of love, "wound the eyes of whoever beholds" Beatrice, and through these "portals" of Being they reach the hearts of the beholders as they at once see and are seen by her. We should note that this moment of union in love between two subjects, as each is the object of the other's gaze, is expanded to include a subject, the *you* of a chorus that includes each one of us, *now*, as subject of this phrase: "you see Love depicted in her face, / there where none may behold her steadily." This is, therefore, a momentary, fleeting and intermittent epiphany of Love manifested in the beloved's face, for, as we have already noted, "human kind cannot bear very much reality"!

For brevity's sake I shall now read a few more selections of the figure of the gaze from *The New Life*, before commenting on its presence in the sonnet, "Oltre la spera che più larga gira" ("Beyond the sphere that circles widest"), which immediately precedes the last chapter of this work. From the sonnet "Ne li occhi porta la mia donna Amore," in chapter XXI:

> In her eyes my lady brings Love,
> whereby is ennobled whatever she looks upon;
> where she passes, everyone toward her turns,
> and whoever she greets trembles at heart,
> so that, lowering the eyes, one grows all pale,
> and for each fault one then sighs:
> . . .
> and one is praised who sees her first.
> What she seems when she but smiles
> cannot be described or held in mind,
> so much is she a miracle new and gentle.

In Dante's commentary to these verses we read: "In the first part I say how through her power she makes noble all that she beholds, and this is tantamount to saying that she brings Love forth into potentiality where he is not; in the second I say how she brings Love forth into actuality in the hearts of all those whom she beholds . . . Of her wonderful smile . . . I do not say how it works in the hearts of others, because memory cannot retain her smile or its operation."

In chapter XXVI we find this sonnet, which, like every middle school student in Italy, I had to learn by heart:

So gentle and so honest appears
my lady when she greets others
that every tongue, trembling, becomes mute,
and eyes dare not look at her.
She goes hearing herself praised,
benevolently clothed in humility,
and seems a thing come down
from heaven to earth to reveal miraculousness.
She appears so pleasing to whoever beholds her
that she sends through the eyes a sweetness to the
    heart,
which no one understands who does not feel it:
and it seems that from her lips moves
a spirit, soothing and full of love,
that goes saying to the soul: Sigh.

It is now time to comment on the sonnet, that, again, speaks of a sigh, in chapter XLII:

Beyond the sphere that circles widest
penetrates the sigh that issues from my heart:
a new intelligence, which Love,
weeping, places in him, draws him ever upward.
When he arrives where he desires,
He sees a lady, who receives honor,
And so shines that, because of her splendor,
the pilgrim spirit gazes upon her.
He sees her such that when he tells me of it,
I do not understand him, so subtly does he speak
to the sorrowing heart, which makes him speak.
I know that he speaks of that gentle one,

for he often remembers Beatrice,
so that I understand him well, dear ladies.

A close reading will reveal a process of transformation
of a key term, introduced in the prose, namely of Dante's
thought: first into the figure of the "sigh" and then in the
"new intelligence," placed in it by the weeping "Love" as a
Prime Mover; and then in the figure of the "pilgrim spirit."
The familiar, conventional opposition between thought,
and hence discursive reason, language, on one hand, and
the unique language of the sigh, on the other hand, is here
transcended, by virtue of a kind of symbiosis. It seems to
me that the key word here is, indeed, transcendence, which
at first, in Dante's journey, has been marked by a nostalgia
for a beatitude promised by Beatrice's greeting in a
horizontal, temporal dimension; and later, especially
toward the end of the *New Life*, this transcendence, more
properly has taken the form of a vertical movement, at first
foreshadowed by a nostalgia for the future, and now, at the
very end of that journey, we discover that it is experienced
as a nostalgia for the eternal now of Paradise, embodied in
the figure of the sigh, which is transformed into the pilgrim
spirit that, as a *persona*, or, as its etymology tells us, as a
mask of Dante poet and lover, now *sees a lady, who receives
honor in Heaven,* and *because of her splendor, it gazes upon
her.* This vision of Beatrice is ineffable. It transcends
language, and thus understanding. As such, it awaits, or
points to another vision, as we find announced, but not yet
represented, in the last chapter of *The New Life:*

> After this sonnet there appeared to me a
> wonderful vision, in which I saw things that
> made me resolve to write no more of this blessed
> one until I could more worthily treat of her. And
> to arrive at that, I apply myself as much as I can,
> as she truly knows. So that, if it be pleasing to
> Him for whom all things live that my life may last
> for some years, I hope to say of her what was
> never said of any other woman. And then may it
> please Him who is the Lord of courtesy that my

soul may go to see the glory of this lady: namely, that blessed Beatrice, who in glory gazes upon the face of Him *qui est per omnia secula benedictus* [who is for all ages blessed].

As it is generally known, here Dante announces what later in his life, during his exile from Florence, will write, in his *Commedia,* of his vision of Hell, Purgatory, and Paradise, from which I shall now select a few salient examples of his poetics of the gaze.

II

In the first canto of *Inferno* Dante the poet constructs this scene of his encounter—in his role as the wayfarer or pilgrim—with the soul of the ancient poet Virgil, at the moment when a she-wolf forces him to lose hope of climbing a hill, that, allegorically, foreshadows the mountain of Purgatory, at whose summit lies the Garden of Eden. This scene takes shape as the wayfarer is retreating down toward the dark wood of sin:

> While I retreated down to lower ground,
> before my eyes there suddenly appeared
> one who seemed faint because of the long silence.
> When I saw him in that vast desert,
> "Have pity on me," were the words I cried,
> "whatever you may be—a shade, a man."
> (Inf. 1.61-66)

This scene emerges the moment the pilgrim is completely powerless, alone with his terror. It is important to note that here Dante does not say that Virgil appeared to him or that he saw Virgil coming to his rescue. Here we find two separate and distinct scenes that are dialectically related. In the first the new action that intersects the wayfarer's retreat towards the dark wood is initially represented as an objective *happening* (as we have already noted in *The New Life*) before it is perceived as an *event that it is seen.* Dante writes: "dinanzi a li occhi mi si fu offerto / chi per lungo silenzio parea fioco" ("before my eyes there suddenly appeared /one who seemed faint because of the long silence"). In the scene that follows, the act of seeing is expressed by the verb *vidi* (I saw). This reveals the subject's deeper awareness of what appears before his eyes, which, significantly, is intimately related to a keener perception of the background, the scenic dimension, within which the object appears—"lo gran diserto" ("the vast desert"). Of even greater consequence is the deep connection of this seeing with the assertion of the subject as he utters the words "*Miserere* di me" ("Have pity on me"). These are the first words of the most famous of the Penitential Psalms (number 51 of the Vulgate). They are addressed by the Psalmist to God ("*Miserere mei, Deus*"). Against the starkness of the *gran diserto* (the "vast desert") we see two equally stark figures, standing one before the other in absolute nakedness, one essentially, absolutely defined by his misery, and the other, correspondingly, by his pity, the *misericordia* that such pity calls forth. The poetic power of the words "*Miserere* di me" is directly dependent on the perception, or vision of the "shade or living man," *as other*, and not as many *dantisti* still continue to read, as Virgil. This entire scene would collapse if we imagined that the wayfarer's words were addressed to Virgil, or worse, to Virgil-as-the-allegory-of-Reason! The wayfarer's misery calls forth and invocation for help addressed to *anyone* who can *act* like God, Who, as totally Other, remains hidden. As Hans Urs von Balthasar writes,

> [God] "plays" through human beings and ultimately *as* a human being . . . The good which takes place in God's action really is affected by the world's ambiguity and remains a hidden good. This good is something *done;* it cannot be contemplated in pure "aesthetics" nor proved and demonstrated in pure "logic." It takes place nowhere but on the world stage—which is every living person's present moment—and its destiny

is seen in the drama of world history that is continually unfolding.[16]

Another fitting commentary are Karl Kerényi's remarks, as he cites Pliny the Elder: "*Deus est mortali iuvare mortalem.* The fact that man helps another man, is God to man."[17] A similar view is expressed by Levinas in his *Of God Who Comes to Mind:* "The idea-of-the-Infinite-in-me—or my relation to God—comes to me in the concreteness of my relation to the other man, in the sociality which is my responsibility for my neighbor."[18] In light of these remarks we now have a deeper understanding of Dante's representation of the scene of his encounter with the Other, which reveals the fine distinction between what is perceived as a *happening* that appears *to his eyes* and *his seeing it as an event* that takes place *for him*, awakening in him a deeper awareness of his being in the world, especially his encounter of and relationship with the Other.

In the second canto of *Inferno*, which, together with the first canto, constitutes the poem's Prologue, there is a scene in which we find Virgil's revelation to Dante the wayfarer of Beatrice's appearance to him in Limbo, where, within a "noble castle," in "a meadow of green flowering plants," he dwells along with noble spirits from antiquity, including Homer, Plato and Aristotle, and many others. Here is a selection from this episode:

> I was among those souls who are suspended;
> a lady called to me, so blessed, so lovely
> that I implored to serve at her command.
> Her eyes surpassed the splendor of the stars;

---

[16] Hans Urs von Balthasar, *Theo-Drama: Theological Dramatic Theory,* trans. Graham Harrison (San Francisco: Ignatius Press, 1988), 19.

[17] Kark Kerényi, "Theos e Mythos," in *Il problema della demitizzazione,* ed. Enrico Castelli (Padova: Cedam, 1961), 39, my translation. See Pliny, *Nat. Hist.,* 2.18.

[18] Emmanuel Levinas, *Of God Who Comes to Mind,* trans. Bettina Bergo (Stanford: Stanford University Press, 1998), xiv.

and she began to speak to me---so gently
and softly—with angelic voice. She said:
    O spirit of the courteous Mantuan,
whose fame is still a presence in the world
and shall endure as long as the world lasts,
        my friend, who has not been the friend of
            fortune,
is hindered in his path along that lonely
hillside; he has been turned aside by terror.
. . .
    Go now; with your persuasive word, with all
that is required to see that he escapes,
bring help to him, that I may be consoled.
    For I am Beatrice who send you on;
I come from where I most long to return;
Love prompted me, that Love which makes me
    speak.
                                            (*Inf.* II.52-72)

After Virgil's response to Beatrice's pleadings on
behalf of Dante, and after she reveals to him that she was
sent by Lucy, who was sent by Mary, who, as it is implied,
was sent by God, Who remains hidden, Virgil evokes for
Dante this scene:

    "When she had finished with her words to
        me,
    she turned her gleaming, tearful eyes,
    which only made me hurry all the more.
        And, just as she had wished, I came to you:
    I snatched you from the path of the fierce beast
    that barred the shortest way up the fair
        mountain."
                                            (*Inf.* II.115-120)

Once again Dante the poet invites us to discover and be
moved by the creative power of his poetics of the gaze. The
incipit, or beginning of the episode of Beatrice's meeting
with Virgil took shape with the luminous image of
Beatrice's "eyes" that "surpassed the splendor of the stars",

75

and the *explicit,* or ending of the episode, we now see
expressed, before *our eyes,* by the luminous image of
Beatrice's "gleaming, tearful eyes." Again we witness the
power of the gaze to at once complement and transcend,
with its silent language, the power of words, of language, in
this case—as a sign of Beatrice's love for her "friend. . . and
not the friend of fortune"—to move Virgil to action. As we
are implicitly invited to see side by side the two images of
the splendor of Beatrice's eyes, we are moved by the shift
from the pure light or splendor of her eyes to the light that
coincides with her eyes filled with tears, and especially by
the subtle motion of her eyes: "li occhi lucenti lagrimando
volse" (a verse marked by the predominance of the 'liquid'
consonant '*l*', and thus, to use a technical term, by the
creative power of phonosymbolism). It is this movement of
the "gleaming, tearful eyes" of Beatrice, directed at Virgil,
that makes him "hurry all the more" to save Dante the
wayfarer, who, with fear and trembling, is facing the
irreducible fact of evil embodied by the she-wolf, as he
along with all human beings face in the "journey of our
life." Charles S. Singleton offers this illuminating
commentary on the subtle movement of Beatrice's "tearful
eyes":

> *Volgere* [to turn, in Italian] often is used to signify
> a turning of the attention rather than a bodily
> movement. Beatrice was looking at Virgil before,
> as she spoke to him; it is only now that her eyes
> fill with tears, as she continues to face toward him
> and urges to proceed to the rescue of the wayfarer
> on the dark slope. It is this that makes Virgil more
> eager to do her command.[19]

III

I shall now comment on another example of Dante's
poetics of the gaze, focusing on the episode of Ciacco, a

---

[19] Charles S. Singleton, *Inferno: Text and Commentary*
(Princeton: Princeton University Press, 1977), 38.

Florentine known for his gluttony, in *Inferno* VI. The problematic relationship between inordinate passion and the friendship that defines one's connection to the community or *polis* and ultimately to God and His City is elaborated in this episode. The landscape within which Virgil and Dante the wayfarer move symbolizes the destructive power of a natural desire or passion that has been perverted (we should recall that in Dante's Inferno dwell souls of sinners who have died unrepented):

> I am in the third circle, filled with cold,
> unending, heavy, and accursed rain;
> its measure and its kind are never changed.
> > Gross hailstones, water gray with filth, and
> > snow
> come streaking down across the shadowed air;
> the earth, as it receives that shower, stinks.
> > > > *(Inf.* VI.7-12)

As we see Dante and Virgil walk across the shades of the gluttons, setting their "soles upon / their empty images that seem like persons" (vv. 34-36), we are struck by the suddenness with which one of the shades emerges from the multitude of those who share his fate, lying on the filthy ground under a heavy rain, as soon as he sets his eyes on the two wayfarers:

> And all those spirits lay upon the ground,
> except for one who set erect as soon
> as he caught sight of us in front of him.
> > "O you who are conducted through Hell,"
> he said to me, "recall me, if you can;
> for you, before I was unmade, were made."
> > And I to him: "It is perhaps your anguish
> that snatches you out of my memory,
> so that it seems that I have never seen you.
> > But tell me who you are, you who are set
> in such a dismal place, such punishment—
> if other pains are more, none's more disgusting."
> > And he to me: "Your city—one so full

of envy that its sack has always spilled—
that city held me in the sunlit life.
    The name your citizens gave me was Ciacco;
and for the damning sin of gluttony,
as you can see, I languish in the rain."
(Inf. VI.37-54)

As soon as we observe that the soul addresses Dante alone, pointedly challenging him with a touch of self-irony to be recognized, while he instead declares that he recognizes his interlocutor as a fellow-Florentine, we interpret his sudden awakening, in a sense his "coming alive" or "into being," against the backdrop of the other unnamed shades that remain supine, "*as soon / as he caught sight*" of Dante and Virgil," as an unmistakable sign of the solicitude, or natural friendship that binds one to his fellow-citizen. He reveals his identity as being inextricably linked to his city and its citizens, who named him Ciacco, a nickname meaning "hog," but also an abbreviation of the name Giacomo. Thus, Ciacco is both the good citizen Giacomo and an undignified glutton or "hog." It is notable that Ciacco, before identifying himself, reveals his love for his city by identifying, from an ethical and political perspective, the ills ("the envy") that perverts its order. He does this adopting a language that, allusively, is that of a glutton, whose own "sack has always spilled." Thus, as he judges his city, he is also judging himself. In him coexist Giacomo, the original good citizen, and the "hog." Hence, in this inner conflict, we discover a measure of his anguish and his hell.

    We can see in a sharper light at once Ciacco's authentic love for his city and the perversion of this love by his sin of gluttony in this closing scene evoked by Dante the narrator:

"But when you have returned to the sweet
    world,
I pray, recall me to men's memory:
I say no more to you, answer no more."
    Then his straight gaze grew twisted and awry;
he looked at me awhile, then bent his head;

he fell as low as all his blind companions.

(*Inf.* VI.88-93)

In his "prayer" to Dante to be remembered by the citizens of Florence, nostalgically identified with the "sweet world," we catch one last glimpse of Ciacco-as-Giacomo, the good, loving citizen. Then, in the image of the silent Ciacco, whose "straight gaze"—as a last vestige of his friendly "face to face" connection to Dante the fellow citizen—"grew twisted and awry," we discern one who has lost his original identity as a member of the city-state of Florence. As we see him turn away, speechless, from Dante, we are reminded of Ciacco the "hog" who is about to be blinded by his gluttony: as in a tavern scene on earth, he now appears eternally bent on "filling his sack" until "it spills," as he joins all the other blind gluttons, who constitute a false image of and a perversion of a true community and a true *polis*.

With Dante the wayfarer and the author we experience the tragic emotions of pity and terror, as our minds are arrested by and united to Ciacco's suffering, witnessing the coexistence in him of his longing to be a good, loving citizen of Florence and of his perverting such longing and such love with his gluttony. This sin, like all sins (though to different degrees), in Dante's ethical and theological perspective, has profound social consequences. It stifled Ciacco's natural desire to contribute to the common good of his city, and therefore to be a good citizen and a good friend, in his community and ultimately, as a friend of God, in the celestial city. The poet gives special expression to the point of intersection of such longing with the sense of having been exiled from his beloved city for his sin by focusing on the liminal, suspended moment, full of undefinable anguish, of Ciacco's final gaze, directed at the Other, his fellow-citizen and friend, *beyond words*, at once revealing and concealing "what meaning cannot convey," to borrow a phrase from Hans Ulrich Gumbrecht.[20] At the

---

[20] Hans Ulrich Gumbrecht, *Production of Presence: What Meaning Cannot Convey* (Stanford: Stanford University Press, 2004), 108.

moment of Ciacco's turning away from Dante, his straight gaze becoming "twisted and awry," the poet pointedly recalls, "he looked at me awhile."

IV

I will now comment briefly on the episode of Dante's and Virgil's encounter of the souls of the envious, who are expiating their sin on the Secod Terrace of the Mountain of Purgatory, focusing on the following scene evoked by Dante:

> I opened—wider than before—my eyes:
> I looked ahead of me, and I saw shades
> with cloaks that shared their color with the rocks
> . . .
>> Those souls—it seemed—were cloaked in coarse haircloth;
> another's shoulder served each shade as prop,
> and all of them were bolstered by the rocks:
>> so do the blind who have to beg appear
> on pardon days to plead for what they need,
> each bending his head back and toward the other,
>> that all who watch feel—quickly—pity's touch
> not only through the words that would entreat
> but through the sight, which can—no less—beseech.
>> And just as, to the blind, no sun appears,
> so to the shades—of whom I now speak—here
> the light of heaven would not give itself;
>> for iron wire pierces and sews up
> the lids of all those shades, as untamed hawks
> are handled, lest, too restless, they fly off.
>> It seemed to me a gross discourtesy
> for me, going, to see and not be seen . . .
>> *(Purg.* XIII.46-48; 58-74)

Clearly, here emphasis is given to the creative power of sight, of the gaze experienced by the wayfarer—as he opens his eyes "wider than before—in sharp contrast to the state of the penitent souls whose eyes are shut, with their lids sewn with iron wire. With Dante and Virgil we now experience the negation of the gaze and its power to express love. In their life's journey these shades envied their neighbor's happiness, rejoicing in their downfall. The first image before Dante's eyes is that of shades whose cloaks—like those of the blind on earth—are not bright but as dull as the rocks that function as a background against which those shades, therefore, appear indistinct, as they "shared their color with the rocks." These shades are now expiating their sin, which, morally and spiritually made them blind in their relationship with their fellow human beings. In fact, we cannot speak of a relationship, which implies a degree of intersubjectivity, of shared experience of each other's goodness, each open to the uniqueness of the face, which as Levinas has written, "is alone in translating transcendence. A transcendence that is inseparable from the ethical *circumstances* of the responsibility for the other."[21] Significantly, Dante feels that it is a gross discourtesy for him to see these shades and not be seen. In contrast to what the envious experienced in life, Dante—as suggested earlier with the analogy of the envious-as-the blind on "pardon day"—now feels pity for the blind shades, which, significantly, can be expressed not only "through words that would entreat / but through the sight, which can—no less—beseech."

V

It is now time to turn our attention to a few examples of Dante's poetics of the gaze that informs the third *cantica: Paradiso.* For brevity's sake, before I comment, at some length, on the 23rd canto of *Paradiso,* I will cite a few passages in which the figure of the gaze shines through the page. In canto II we read of Dante's ascent to the Moon, with Beatrice as his new guide (Virgil has gone back to Limbo after he, with Dante and Statius, have entered the

---

[21] Emmanuel Levinas, *Outside the Subject*, trans. Michael B. Smith (Stanford: Stanford University Press, 1994), 94.

Earthly Paradise, which lies at the summit of the Mountain of Purgatory):

> The thirst that is innate and everlasting—
> thirst for the godly realm—bore us away
> as swiftly as the heavens that you see,
>> Beatrice gazed upward. I watched her.
> But in a span perhaps no longer than
> an arrow takes to strike, to fly, to leave
>> the bow, I reached a place where I could see
> that something wonderful drew me; and she
> from whom my need could not be hidden, turned
>> to me (her gladness matched her loveliness):
> "Direct your mind to God in gratefulness,"
> she said; "He has brought us to the first star."
>> (*Par.* II.19-30)

In canto IV, still in the Heaven of the Moon, we read:

> [Then] Beatrice looked at me with eyes so
>> full
> of sparks of love, eyes so divine that my
> own force of sight was overcome, took flight,
>> and eyes downcast, I almost lost my senses.
>> (*Par.* IV.139-142)

Canto X opens with these verses that invite the reader to contemplate the Wisdom of the Triune God and the harmony of Creation—a fitting introduction to Dante's and Beatrice's ascent to the Fourth Heaven, the Sphere of the Sun (here the Power is God the Father, Who gazes upon His Son, Jesus, with the Love, i.e., the Holy Spirit that both "breath"):

> Gazing upon His Son with the Love which
> One and the Other breath eternally,
> the Power—first and inexpressible—
>> made everything that wheels through mind
>>> and space
> so orderly that one who contemplates

that harmony cannot but taste of Him.
    Then, reader, lift your eyes with me to see
the high wheels; gaze directly at that part
where the one motion strikes against the other;
    and there begin to look with longing at
the Master's art, which in Himself he loves
so much that his eye never parts from it.
                                    (*Par.* X.1-12)

VI

Let us now turn our attention to canto XXIII, where the episode of Beatrice's smile is woven into the theo-drama of the Triumphs of Christ and of Mary. I will first cite the last verses of the preceding canto, which constitute the ground for the poetics of the gaze that informs the 23rd canto:

    And all the seven heavens showed to me
their magnitudes, their speeds, the distances
of each from each. The little threshing floor
    that so incites our savagery was all—
from hills to river mouths—revealed to me
while I wheeled with the eternal Gemini.
    My eyes then turned again to the fair eyes.
                                    (*Par.*XXII.148-154)

The closing verse of *Paradiso* XXII speaks of a significant moment that at once advances and arrests the action: "My eyes then turned again to the fair eyes." The turn of the pilgrim's gaze from the seven planets circling below his feet, and, specifically, from "the little threshing floor / that incites our savagery" to Beatrice's beautiful eyes, may at first be interpreted as a sign of the pilgrim's total detachment from and indeed negation of our earth and the whole visible universe. Yet, in the light of the preceding remarks, it seems at least plausible that, at a certain level of his consciousness, he is aware of the proportion between the special creative force of the beauty of Beatrice's eyes and that of the beauty of the universe. In short, the turning of his gaze from the order and beauty of the world that gave him an imperfect delight to the beauty of Beatrice's eyes that suggests the perfecting of that delight, while stressing an upward movement of transcendence, still constitutes an action that, dialectically, calls forth the counter-assertion of a downward pull toward our world. Needless to say, in this moment of suspense, which at once joins and separates the end of *Paradiso* XXII and the beginning of canto XXIII, as the pilgrim gazes into the beautiful eyes of the beloved, thus arresting the preceding upward thrust of his glance, the opposition between time and eternity, and heaven and earth, is still hidden and only dialectically implied by the sequence of scenes that have led to the present one.

The opening scene of *Paradiso* XXIII (1-12), evoked by the vehicle of the bird simile, as it both announces and interprets the actual scene described by the tenor, of Beatrice's expectant gaze fixed upon the Zenith, represents an important first solution and transcendence of the opposition between heaven and earth we just mentioned:

> As does the bird, among beloved branches,
>   when, through the night that hides things from us, she
> has rested near the nest of her sweet fledglings
>   and, on an open branch, anticipates
> the time when she can see their longed-for faces
> and find the food with which to feed them—chore
>   that pleases her, however hard her labors—
> as she awaits the sun with warm affection,
> steadfastly watching for the dawn to break:
>   so did my lady stand, erect, intent,
> turned toward that part of heaven under which
> the sun is given to less haste . . .

We now experience a sudden return to the familiar world of nature, with its order and beauty. The pilgrim's perspective, as he fixes his eyes on the eyes of Beatrice, is abandoned by the poet in his attempt to give form to the present paradisal scene. In sharp contrast to "the little threshing floor / that incites our savagery," at least a part of this insignificant and violent world is now portrayed as significant, harmonious, and beautiful, in and of itself, but also *significant* in the larger sense of pointing, by analogy, to the ultimate, transcendent reality, with its order and beauty, as well as its mystery. This sudden shift of focus that the narrator shares with his reader is remarkable, if we recall that he, more than the pilgrim who responded with a bitter smile, expressed his disdain for our globe's "meager image": "I approve / that judgement as the best, which holds this earth / to be the least" (*Par.* XXII.136-137).

As soon as our attention is directed to Beatrice, we are drawn into the scene of the pilgrim whose gaze is fixed on his beloved: "as I saw her in longing and suspense, / I grew to be as one who, while he wants / what is not his, is satisfied with hope" (13-15). The focus is now on the dramatic transformation brought about in the pilgrim by his mimetic response to the beloved's act of longing expectation: now he experiences at once the desire or love for something that is not present and the satisfaction in hoping for its manifestation. Thus he experiences faith, which is "the substance of the things we hope for, and the evidence of things not seen," as he will affirm in *Paradiso* XXIV, paraphrasing St. Paul's Letter to the Hebrews (11.1), in answer to St. Peter's question, "what is faith?". Here emphasis is also given to the universal human condition of longing expectation, as the pronoun *quei* ("one who") in the phrase "I grew to be as one who. . .").

Once again, the poet has cast a glance toward our world as he interprets the secret transformation that has now occurred within the pilgrim: the opposition between the perverted beauty of "the little threshing floor / that so incites our savagery" and the beauty of the universe, which earlier he had "organized," is now transformed into the expectation of that which will resolve it—an expectation that we saw adumbrated as a motivational force in the scene that represented that opposition.

The shift from expectation to vision is almost instantaneous, suggesting the transcendent nature of the faith (and hope) implicit in that expectation and of God's answer to it (16-21):

> But time between one and the other *when*
> was brief—I mean the *when* of waiting and
> of seeing heaven grow more radiant.
>   And Beatrice said : "There you see the troops
> of the triumphant Christ—and all the fruits
> ingathered from the turning of these spheres!"

This scene marks the beginning of the second segment or act of the canto (16-45), which contains the vision of Christ's triumph. As it introduces this vision, it reveals the intimate relashionship between light (and hence beauty), which is what the pilgrim first apprehends, and the good that Beatrice unveils to Dante. As the action of this vision unfolds, we observe that beauty as light is at once the source and goal for the beholders, as well as the source and goal of the poetic representation. And within the economy of this representation, it is once again Beatrice who, with her heightened beauty, mediates between that source (and goal) and Dante, protagonist and poet (22-24):

> It seemed to me her face was all aflame,
> and there was so much gladness in her eyes—
> I am compelled to leave it undescribed.

As Beatrice's transfigured face and joyful eyes mirror Christ's radiance and the radiance of the blessed souls, they reveal through beauty the paradoxical hidden revelation of the Incarnation and its fruitfulness in human history. The faith represented in Beatrice, as she gazes into the radiant Christ whom she has longingly awaited, is revealed by her growing brighter and brighter as she is transformed into the image she reflects. Thus, she is no longer only a mediator or a *sign* that *points* to Christ and the mystery of Incarnation, and, correspondingly, to the mystery of faith, but has become herself an ineffable source and goal of Dante's vision, to a degree that surpasses all previous manifestations of her mysterious goodness and beauty, including her equally mysterious salvific effect on Dante, as lover and poet, which can be traced within the *Commedia* and also back to the *Vita Nuova* (*The New Life*).

In perfect consonance with the pilgrim's experience of the mystery of faith as manifested *through* and *in* Beatrice, the narrator "leaps" into silence which is paradoxically expressed by his declaration that he cannot speak of this experience. As we turn our attention from the pilgrim's vision of Beatrice's transfigured face to his vision of Christ's triumph, which the poet introduces with the famous simile of Trivia (a term applied to Diana, the goddess of the Moon, and hence by Dante to the moon), we experience with the pilgrim the paradoxically creative empty moment or caesura which, although unutterable, at once reveals his inadequacy to fathom the mystery of Beatrice's heightened beauty and the inner transformation arising in him at the sight of that beauty, which enables him to gaze into the new, spiritual sun that shines above him. Thus, Dante, like Beatrice, is transformed by the object of his vision, expressing the theological aesthetics of vision and rapture embodied in these words of St. Paul that we read in his Second Letter to the Corinthians (3.18): "And we, with our unveiled faces reflecting like mirrors the brightness of the Lord, all grow brighter and brighter as we are turned into the image that we reflect; this is the work of the Lord who is Spirit."

As we read the Trivia simile, we note that, suddenly, the narrator's voice turns from the declaration of ineffability to fabulation (25-33):

> Like Trivia—at the full moon in clear skies—
> smiling among the everlasting nymphs
> who decorate all reaches of the sky,
>   I saw a sun above a thousand lamps:
> it kindled all of them as does our sun
> kindle the sights above us here on earth;
>   and through its living light the glowing
>   Substance
> appeared to me with such intensity—
> my vision lacked the power to sustain it.

The moment of the pilgrim's fruition of this experience emerges suddenly, without solution of continuity, with these words that Beatrice addresses to Dante (46-48):

> "Open your eyes and see what I now am;
> the things you witnessed will have made you strong
> enough to bear the power of my smile."

In the general economy of Dante's journey, his erotic quest finds fulfillment in the contemplation of the beloved's spiritual beauty, as he, after the "ten year thirst" he has endured, can finally sustain the vision of her "wonderful smile," of which he spoke in the *Vita Nuova* (XXI). Within the economy of the *Commedia* this is the epiphany (which foreshadows the final epiphany of Beatrice's beauty of *Paradiso* XXX, which in turn points to Dante's vision of God, face to face, which marks the end of the poem) of the action whose prologue was represented in *Purgatorio* XXX.73, where Beatrice, in the Earthly Paradise, addressed Dante with these words; "Guardaci ben! Ben son, ben son Beatrice" ("Look here! For I am Beatrice, I am!").

VII

I will now bring my talk to a close, reading the following verses from *Paradiso* XXXIII (76-145), the last canto of the *Commedia*, in which we find represented the last measure of Dante's poetics of the gaze:

> The living ray that I endured was so
> acute that I believe I should have gone
> astray had my eyes turned away from it.
>   I can recall that I, because of this,
> was bolder in sustaining it until
> my vision reached the Infinite Goodness.
>   O grace abounding, through which I presumed
> to set my eyes on the Eternal Light
> so long that I spent all my sight on it!
>   In its profundity I saw—ingathered
> and bound by love into one single volume—

what, in the universe, seems separate, scattered:
    substances, accidents, and dispositions
as if conjoined—in such a way that what
I tell is only rudimentary.
    I think I saw the universal shape
which that knot takes; for, speaking this, I feel
a joy that is more ample. That one moment
    brings more forgetfulness to me than twenty-
five centuries have brought to the endeavor
that startled Neptune with the Argo's shadow!
    So was my mind—completely rapt, intent,
steadfast and motionless—gazing; and it
grew ever more enkindled as it watched.
    Whoever sees that Light is soon made such
that it would be impossible for him
to set aside that Light for other sight;
    because the good, the object of the will,
is fully gathered in that Light: outside
that Light, what there is perfect is defective.
    What little I recall is to be told,
from this point on, in words more weak than those
of one whose infant tongue still bathes at the breast.
    And not because more than one simple
        semblance
was in the Living Light at which I gazed—
for It is always what It was before—
    but through my sight, which as I gazed grew
        stronger,
that sole appearance, even as I altered,
seemed to be changing. In the deep and bright
    essence of that exalted Light, three circles
appeared to me; they had three different colors,
but all of them were of the same dimension;
    one circle seemed reflected by the second,
as rainbow is by rainbow, and the third
seemed fire breathed equally by those two circles.
    How incomplete is speech, how weak, when set
against my thought! And this, to what I saw
is such—to call it little is too much.
    Eternal Light, You only dwell within

Yourself, and only You know You: Self-knowing,
Self-known, You love and smile upon Yourself!
    That circle—which, begotten so, appeared
in You as light reflected—when my eyes
had watched it with attention for some time,
    within itself and colored like itself,
to me seemed painted with our effigy,
so that my sight was set on it completely.
    As the geometer intently seeks
to square the circle, but he cannot reach,
through thought on thought, the principle he needs,
    so I searched that strange sight: I wished to see
the way in which our human effigy
suited the circle and found place in it—
    and my own wings were far too weak for that.
But then my mind was struck by light that flashed
and, with this light, received what it had asked.
    Here force failed my high fantasy; but my
desire and will were moved already—like
a wheel revolving uniformly—by
    the Love that moves the sun and the other stars.

As I pronounce these words that speak of Dante's vision of
God, face to face, I think of them as an answer to Job, who
expressed his longing to see God, face to face, with these
words:

"This I know: that my Redeemer lives,
and he, the Last, will take his stand on earth.
After my awaking, he will set me close to him,
and from my flesh I shall look on God.
He whom I shall see will take my part:
these eyes will gaze on him and find him not aloof."
                            (Job 19.25-27)

GAZE

Peter Booth

There is a very beautiful word in Persian —نظر (*nazar*)—
fairly synonymous with the word "gaze" in English, but
with a far wider range of meanings. For example, to say in
Persian "my nazar is on you" means "I am looking out for
you," or, in contemporary terms, "I've got your back."
However, the sense of a prolonged sight between lover and
Beloved that gaze implies in English is generally lacking in
Hafiz, so spontaneous and ever-changing is the
relationship between these two. Nonetheless, vision, sight,
or "gaze"—if you prefer—is at the center of Hafiz's
cosmology. Simply, the entire thing is built on sight or
appearance, so let's take a look at it.

Hafiz's conception of existence is monotheistic, but
rather than just calling this existence God he also calls it
Love.[1] This existence is an uncreated, infinite existence—
outside the boundaries of time and space. It just is. Being
uncreated it lacks the primary benchmark or reference
point of origin, and without this benchmark or point of
reference it lacks anything that can be measured—that is,
size, space, time, volume, or substance. As Love is infinite,
it is faced with the problem of having to create a situation
allowing it to express its nature as Love. That is, it can't be
love unless it can express itself as love and to do this it has
to have something or someone other than itself to love.
However, as Love is an infinite existence, it is not possible
for it to create or add anything on to itself, for if there were

---

[1] For a short discussion of Love in Islamic mysticism and Hafiz,
see Agu Ashgar Syed-Gohrab, "The Erotic Spirit," in *Hafiz and
the Religion of Love in Classical Persian Poetry*, ed. Leonard
Lewisohn (London: I. B. Tauris, 2010), 109-110.

an empty space allowing for addition, Love would not be infinite; it would be circumscribed by the void where it does not exist, making it finite. There being a lack of space in Love's infinity for the addition of creation, then it must be that creation supplants an area of Love's existence—elbows it out of the way as it were. But, if this were the case, addition would actually be subtraction as a line of demarcation would be drawn separating Love's infinity from its creation and, in the process, Love would lose its infinity and become finite. Hafiz makes it clear that this can never happen, as God, as infinite Love, is in no way limited, affected, or altered by His apparent creation of creation. That is, although He creates creation, His infinity is not lost. Bearing this in mind, let's see how Hafiz describes this creation of apparent separation of Love into lover and Beloved allowing Love to express its true nature as Love. As Hafiz's poetic style is extremely subtle, he peppers allusions to his conception of creation throughout his body of work, so we have to draw these together to arrive at an understanding.

As an entree as to how and why Love creates creation, let's start with the Beloved's cheek, the beauty mark, or mole on it, and the relationship Hafiz establishes between this beauty mark (sounds better than mole) and the pupil of the eye. In the process, we will also encounter Hafiz's referential poetic style wherein referring to and comparing the qualities of one thing establishes, at least in part, the qualities of another.

In this case, nothing is better suited for expressing the infinity of the infinite and how it relates to the finiteness of creation than the pupil of the eye. The eye's pupil is round, minute, and black, yet it is able to contain vast vistas of sight and the effulgence of light. Hafiz makes it clear that the pupil's ability to contain limitless sight is because it is a reflection of the beauty mark on the Beloved's cheek and by doing this, Hafiz establishes this beauty mark as representing all of creation:

سواد لوح بینش را عزیز از بهر آن دارم
که جان را نسخه‌یی باشد ز لوح خال هندویت ۲

I hold
the pupil of
my eye
dear as
it is
a copy of
your
Hindu
beauty mark.

Or:

این نقطهٔ سیاه که آمد مدار نور
عکسی ست در حدیقهٔ بینش ز خال تو

This black
point
that has
become
the orbit
of light
is a
reflection
of your
beauty mark in
the garden
of sight.

Or:

---

² All Persian text is from: حافظ بر اساس نسخه نو یافته بسیر کهن [The Divan of Hafiz (Based on a newly discovered manuscript written around the time of Hafiz)], ed. Sayyed Sadeq Sajjadi and Ali Bahramiyan, with notes and commentary by Kazem Bargnaysi (Tehran: Fekr-e-ruz, 2001).

مدار نقطهء بینش ز خال توست مرا
که قدر گوهر یکدانه گوهری داند

The orbit of
sight of
the pupil of
my eye is
the beauty mark
on your cheek
the value of
a priceless pearl
only a pearl
knows.

To further build this referential context, for the most part,
the Beloved's cheek represents God's (that is Love's)
infinite uncreated being:

یارب به که شاید این نکته که در عالم
رخساره به کس ننمود آن شاهد هر جایی

God
to whom
in the world
can I relate
this point—
the Beloved
who is
everywhere
has not shown
His cheek
to anyone?[3]

Or:

---

[3] Contrasts with the Quranic verse: "Wherever you turn, there is
the face of God" (Quran II: 115).

هر دو عالم یک فروغ روی اوست
گفتمت پیدا و پنهان نیز هم

Both the
worlds are
a ray of
manifestation
from His
cheek I am
telling you
the visible
and the
hidden both.

Additionally, the Beloved's stature is always presented as
being perfectly erect, whereas everything else is curved:

هر سرو که در چمن برآید
در خدمت قامتت نگون باد

May every cypress
that appears in
the garden be
bent in service
to your erect
stature.

Or:

می شکفتم ز طرب ز انکه چو گل بر لب جوی
بر سرم سایهٔ آن سرو سهی بالا بود

In ecstasy like
a rose along
the bank of a
stream I
blossomed
for above me
the shadow of

that erect cypress
appeared.

Also, this erect stature and the Beloved's unmanifest cheek
are compared with one another:

در چمن باد بهاری ز کنار گل و سرو
به هواداری آن عارض و قامت برخاست

Out of desire
for that cheek
and that erect
stature a spring
breeze arose in
the meadow from
beside the rose
and the cypress.

Now consider this couplet:

روز ازل از کلک تو یک قطره سیاهی
بر سوی مه افتاد که کن حل مسایل

On the
day before
the beginning
of time
a black drop
fell from
your pen
onto
the moon
as the solution
to your
problem.

I believe the problem mentioned here is two things—
first, how to create separation so that there can be a lover-
Beloved relationship and also how to create some degree of

relativity, measure or reflection so that the Beloved may be
made aware of His infinite attributes as is seen here:

بعد از این روی من و آینهٔ وصف جمال
که در آن جا خبر از جلوه ذاتم دادند

> From now on I
> will gaze into
> the mirror reflecting
> His face for
> there I was
> informed of
> God's Manifestation.[4]

Now, taking all of this together, and considering again
that it is not possible for an infinite existence to create
anything as to do so would actually be an act of destruction
rather than creation—that is, existence would lose its
infinity—it becomes clear that Love as the creator solves
this problem by curving or bending its effulgence, much as
clear light passing through a prism is bent and produces the
illusion of colored substances. The black ink drop on the
moon, the pupil of the eye, and the beauty mark on the
Beloved's cheek, as all three are black and spherical, suggest
that the greater the curving of the effulgence of Love, the
greater the darkness, the greater the relativity, and the
greater the separation, as one would expect if this reading
holds true. This increasingly greater curvature spirals down
into less and less effulgence until we arrive at the symbol for
all of creation—the black drop falling onto the moon or the
beauty mark on the Beloved's cheek. These black drops
carry this conceit to its height as, being spherical their
curvature is complete, and in being black there is an
apparent absence of light. If this is the case, Love's creation

---

[4] Hossein-Ali Heravi, in *A Commentary on the Ghazals of Hafiz*
(Tehran: Nashr-e Now Publishing Company, 1989), mentions
that the "mirror of your beauty" and the Beloved's cheek are one
and the same.

has to be a type of optical illusion and not a real existence.
As seen here, Hafiz says this is so:

سبز است در و دشت بیا تا نگذاریم
دست از سر آبی که جهان جمله سراب است

>Verdure spreads
>through the
>valleys and
>the fields,
>come, don't
>waste the
>chance to be
>satiated with
>this beauty
>for the world
>is only a
>mirage.

Or:

عرضه کردم دو جهان بر دل کار افتاده
به جز از عشق تو باقی همه فانی دانست

>I presented
>this world
>and the next
>to my
>ripened heart
>it knew
>immediately
>that
>everything
>save your love
>perishes into
>nothing.

(This world being the material world—the next world
being Paradise)

Or:

منّت سدره و طوبی ز پی سایه مکش

که چو خوش بنگری ای سرو روان این همه نیست

For the
sake of
shade
do not be
under the
obligation
of the sidra
and tuba
trees for
when Oh
flowing cypress
you look closely
all of this is
nothing.[5]

To return to an overview for a moment, as Love is the only existence—that is the primal force— it is not possible for Love to express anything that is not its nature as Love. Or, to put it another way, whatever Love expresses is an expression of its true nature. It cannot express something that it is not because, as we have seen, in being infinite, it is

---

[5] The sidra and the tuba are sacred trees in Islam. The sidra is the tree under which Mohammed saw the angel Gabriel as mentioned in the Koran. Kazim Bargnysi (in حافظ بر اساس نسخه نو یافته بسیر کهن on p. 102) mentions: "According to the traditions of Islam, it is a lote tree in the seventh heaven in the extremities of Paradise that they say is the 'first world and the last' and which it is not possible to go higher than . . . Whatever is connected to it is from the hidden world. It is also the limit of the ascension of Gabriel and it is said that no one save for the Prophet of Islam can ascend higher than it . . . According to the traditions of Islam, the Tuba Tree is a tree in Paradise that God planted with his own hand. This tree is so large that every region of Paradise is a branch of it."

the only thing that exists. Or, simply, in Hafiz's cosmology there is only Love.

Bearing this in mind, let's review for a moment the history of the different presentations of the final manifestation of Love found in classical Persian mysticism.

First you have an eternal sojourn in the ideal, created state of Paradise. For Hafiz Paradise is a bit like a retirement home, where lovers are put out to pasture after Love is through playing with them, or perhaps, if he were alive today, an upscale gated community where the residents pass their days in divinely sanitized boredom. As Love cannot create anything outside of itself, and as love is doing this to express its true nature, then this, if we accept it, must be what Love is. Hafiz totally rejects this.

Then you have the "burst the bubble" conception of the final state of the lover, popularized by one of Rumi's favorite figures where the separation producing the individuality of the lover is compared to the formation of a bubble on the shoreless ocean of God's infinite existence only to have the bubble burst representing the lover's reunion with his source. This is a bit like that heroine of many feminists, the female praying mantis, who, after love making, devourers her mate. If you think about it, this is not a particularly loving end to this thrilling romance, with the Beloved essentially saying, "you were enjoyable to be with for a while but, there is nothing to justify keeping you around for all eternity and I'm moving on, so poof!" Hafiz also rejects this, as why would anyone go to all the trouble to create the miracle of human consciousness only to destroy it in the end? Moreover, in this case Love's essence would be one of rejection, rather than compassionate, loving acceptance.

Bearing this in mind, to begin to arrive at Hafiz's presentation of the final state of the lover, consider these descriptions of the Fall:

زلف او دام است و خالش دانۀ آن دام و من
بر امید دانه یی افتاده ام در دام دوست

His curls are
a trap and
His beauty mark
the seed in
the trap; in
hope of gaining
the seed I have
fallen into
the trap.

Or:

مرغ روحم که همی زد ز سر سدره صفیر
عاقبت دانهء خال تو فکندش در دام

I was a
bird of the
spirit
singing
from the
top of
Gabriel's tree
in paradise
in the
end
I was
cast
into the
trap by
the seed of
the beauty mark
on your
cheek.

Or:

من ملک بودم و فردوس برین جایم بود
آدم آورد درین دیر خراب آبادم

I was an
angel and
paradise was
my abode
it was Adam
who brought
me into
this ancient
flourishing
ruin.

Or:

طایر گلشن قدسم چه دهم شرح فراق
که درین دامگه حادثه چون افتادم

As a bird
of the
holy garden
what description
can I give
of the
separation
I experienced
when I fell
into this
trap of
phenomenon?

At first glance it appears we have encountered a variation on the Judeo-Christian description of the Fall. Reading more closely, however, reveals that Paradise, in Hafiz's conception of existence, is a very inferior, temporary state as it is among the realm of the created, and as such can have no lasting existence. In fact, like the material world, it is absolutely nothing:

جهان چو خلد برین شد به دور سوسن و گل
ولی چه سود که در وی نه ممکن است خلود

In the season
of the lily
and the rose
the world
has become
the highest
paradise
but to what
avail when
there is no
eternity in it?

So the "Fall" of the soul from the realm of Paradise
into the trap around the seed of the beauty mark on the
Beloved's cheek—this beauty mark representing the entire
realm of creation and separation—is actually beneficial, as
the end result for the soul that passes through this realm in
Hafiz's cosmology, as we will see, is Union with God, rather
than a sojourn in the illusory, created realm of paradise that
was the soul's residence before the Fall. Reading further we
find that this black drop, rather than being a sinful flaw as
many might assume, is actually sacred—that is, creation is
sacred—and rather than the soul's fall into this realm being
the result of the expulsion from paradise due to sin, it is
actually because the soul, or God as Love, cannot resist the
beauty of the separation allowing for the lover-Beloved
relationship, represented by falling into the trap of the
beauty mark, as this "Fall" allows Love to express and
experience its true nature by having someone other than
itself to love. In this sense the "Fall" is similar to the
"solution to your problem" mentioned above. Remember,
arriving at an understanding of Love's true nature is what
we are up to.

Elsewhere, Hafiz provides another description of the
Fall, this time using a grain of sand that forms a pearl:

عشق دردنه ست و من غوّاص و دریا میکده
سر فرو بردم در اینجا تا کجا سر بر کنم

Love is
the grain
that forms
the pearl
I am the diver
in the ocean
of the tavern
descending to
see where I
come up.[6]

If there is any relationship between the beauty mark and the grain—each causing the descent of the soul—then it is Love that brings about creation, the soul's descent into creation resulting in the ultimate expression of Love's nature, the creation of an eternal, unique individuality represented by the pearl. The same process is expressed in two different ways.

Returning for a moment to the black drop on the moon and the images associated with it to reinforce our reading. The black drop failing on the moon symbolizes that this black drop is illusory as the moon generates no light by itself, but merely reflects the sun. However, as is seen in many places, the light produced by this black drop and the moon is far greater than that produced by the sun:

خورشید خاوری کند از رشک جامه چاک
گر ماه مهر پرور من در قبا رود

If the love-nurturing
moon fully
adorns itself
the sun of
the east out
of jealously

---

[6] For a discussion of the grain, see Annemarie Schimmel, *A Two-Colored Brocade* (Chapel Hill, University of North Carolina Press, 1992), 60.

will tear open
its cloak.

This couplet also being a beautiful description of the sun rising.

In Hafiz, the end result of the soul's passage through this blackness of separation is the annihilation of just that – any separation. Expressed as فنا *(fana)* by the Persian mystics (as well as Hafiz), these couplets expressing the total annihilation of separate existence and the resulting union between lover and Beloved are among the most beautiful in Hafiz's poetry:[7]

چو شمع صبحدمم شد ز مهر او روشن
که عمر در سر این کار و بار خواهم کرد

Like the candle
of morning
my life
will end
when it
is lit by
the sun of
His compassion.

Or:

آنکه من در جست و جویش خود ندیدم در میان
کس ندیده ست و نبیند مثلش از هر سو ببین

No one
from any
side has
seen the
like of
the One in

---

[7] See Annemarie Schimmel, *Mystical Dimension of Islam* (Chapel Hill: University of North Carolina Press, 2011), 142-145

106

whose search
I have
vanished
from myself.

Or:

به جانت ای بت شیرین من که همچون شمع
شبان تیره مرادم فنای خویشتن است

I swear
by your
soul my
sweet idol
that
like a candle
my only
intention
in these
dark nights
is my own
annihilation.

Or:

گفتم که کی ببخشی بر جان ناتوانم
گفت آن زمان که نبود جان در میانه حایل

I asked,
"when are
you going
to bestow
your grace
on this
weak soul?"
He answered,
"When your
soul
is no longer in
the way."

In Hafiz, after annihilation there remains a speck of dust on the Beloved's foot representing the lover who continues to exist after this annihilation has taken place. This speck, appropriately, contains a light brighter than the sun's:

گرچه خورشید فلک چشم و چراغ عالم است
روشناي بخش چشم اوست خاک پای تو

Although the sun
of the heavens is
the light
of the world
it is the dust
of your feet
that gives
the eye
of the sun
its brightness.

It is natural to think of this couplet as hyperbole, but when we consider it in the over-all context of Hafiz's cosmology, it is obvious that it is not, for the end of the spiritual journey is, as is seen throughout Hafiz, this speck of dust on the door of the Beloved's threshold or on his foot. Yet, despite the minuteness of this speck it contains— as we see in this couplet and elsewhere—an effulgence far brighter than the sun's. Indeed, it is this speck of dust that is the source of the sun's light. To understand how this is possible, let's go back for a moment to the beginning of this talk and consider again that as Love's existence is uncreated, there is no point of reference, or benchmark within it to use to measure anything. Accordingly, from Love's perspective, there is no size or, to put it another way, everything is exactly the same size. This means that a speck of dust on the Beloved's foot is the same size as the universe, which also means that the universe is actually a speck of dust. As Hafiz says:

کمر کوه کم است از کمر مور آنجا

In the realm
of Love the
girth of
a mountain
is less than
the waist of
an ant.

Now, and this is the important part, as everything created is absolutely nothing, nothing created has the power to in anyway divide the infinity of existence. To do this, it would have to be something, and it is not something—it is nothing. What this means is that Infinity is infinitely present in everything in creation no matter how apparently minute that form may be.

So now back to our speck of dust resting on the Beloved's foot. I believe that Hafiz uses a speck of dust in part to express that all of the curved relativity of the illusory creation once producing darkness has been removed with only the uncurved effulgence of God remaining.

A similar expression is found in another of Hafiz's vast metaphors—that of circumference and pivot. As Hafiz presents it, one circumference's pivot is another pivot's circumference and this continuum extends in both directions to infinity with no member of the continuum— from the view point of Reality—being different in size from another, and with every member fully containing, or, better yet, unable to limit Love's infinity. So the pivot cannot be a point relative to or defined by a circumference. The pivot can only be an infinite, uncreated "point" in the limitless existence of Love, imbibed with all of the attributes associated with this—that is, with no volume, size or substance, uncircumscribed by anything or shoreless—and the circumference can only be the turning of all that appears to exist by the curving or bending of Love's effulgence, but, as all of this is nothing, with no ability to in anyway limit or circumvent the pivot. This pivot-circumference relationship is often used to express the state of the God-

Realized soul who has one foot in Reality and the other in illusion. When considering this, we again arrive at two of Hafiz's favorite metaphoric constructs we mentioned before—the perfectly erect stature of the Beloved, most often symbolized by the cypress—representing the pivot, or قطب (*qutub*, "pole or axis") compared with the curved form of everything created, and also the point or "pivot" of infinite sight in the center of the black pupil of the eye:

دل چو پرگار به هر سو دورانی میزد
وندر آن دایره سرگشتهٔ پا بر جا بود

The heart is
like a compass
spinning in every
direction and in
that whirling
circle it has a
foot as a pivot.

Or to put it another way, the challenge in Hafiz's cosmology is for the finite to contain infinity while remaining finite, and for the infinite to manifest within the finite while remaining infinite. That is, for infinite light to manifest in the depths of limitless darkness, without dissolving this darkness into light, as we have seen with the pupil of the eye. If at any time the immeasurably subtle structure of this relationship between the infinite and the finite and between light and darkness dissolves, the beauty mark on the Beloved's cheek will disappear and you will no longer have the illusory shell of creation producing the pearl of an infinite individuality, and Love's problem will not be solved.[8]

To review for a moment, to achieve the lover's God-realized state, God creates an illusory separation within His limitless unity, dividing Himself into lover and Beloved, so that love can experience its true nature through expressing

---

[8] For a description of darkness within light and light within darkness, see Schimmel, *A Two-Colored Brocade*, 144.

love. He creates this separation by curving His effulgence, this curving providing relativity, volume and substance, and in the process creating an apparent "other." Again, as an analogy, think of pure light passing through a prism creating a "mirage." God then annihilates this curving and substance, and lover and Beloved are reunited. In Hafiz, this annihilation is the annihilation of the relativity and curving that brings the lover into existence; it is not the annihilation of the lover's individuality that his passing through this mirage creates. The final state of Love's expression, then, is that the individuality of the lover is maintained after annihilation.

Now it appears we finally have arrived at the conception of Love in Hafiz's poetry. Yet, having arrived at this, we find there is no stasis, or eternal state of rest, as many might expect. In fact everything—including this reunited God-realized state—exists within the realm of Love's limitless and unceasing creativity. When we consider this, it becomes obvious that Love is not going to create— indeed cannot create—anything that is not a pure expression of its nature as nothing other than Love exists. This takes us, I believe, to an understanding of how it is possible to have more than one infinite existence—in fact an infinite number of infinite existences. Love, of course, will want to give everything it has to this created being, as limitless giving is Love's basic nature. So, essentially, Love will want its created lover to have all that it has, including the most priceless possession of all, an infinite, unconditional, unique existence, as this is all that it has. For Love to want it to have anything less than this would make the unconditional, infinite giving of Love conditional and finite. And Hafiz makes it clear that finite, conditional giving can never be a part of Love. That is, you cannot give a part of the infinite. In Love you can only give the Infinite, as Love has nothing to do with the finite as the finite is nothing and does not exist as we have seen. Or, to put it another way, you cannot give nothing even if you are God. Now, the created being that has gained a complete and separate individuality by passing through the sacred darkness of creation is also nothing other than perfect and complete Love. So it too will want to give everything it has—that is its very existence as this is all that it has—to its Beloved. So, essentially, there are now two Beloveds and two lovers, each lost in the limitless giving of each to the other. Yet, despite this limitless giving—no matter how infinite this giving becomes—each continues to exist.

I believe we have now come full circle, having started out presenting Hafiz's cosmology wherein no creation can take place as it is impossible to add on to the infinite, to the "creation" of an eternal real existence of unlimited individuality or "other," this individuality having been produced by the soul passing through the curved illusion of a "created" mirage. What we now have is a qualified conception of the immeasurable nature of Love, qualified conceptions being the best we can arrive at. Meaning that love's infinity before a "new" individuality will not be divided or demarcated, but will remain unlimited not just because in being uncreated Love lacks the point of origin, this point of origin establishing the demarcating force of relativity and all that comes with it—time, space, volume, substance and anything that can be measured—and not just because the new, created individually, in having gone through the curved mirage of creation followed by فنا (fana—the annihilation of this curved relativity) also lacks the same, but also because love's infinite giving, combined with the infinite humility Love experiences from the accompanying infinite receiving, will never allow for anything measurable in the infinity of Love to remain. Here we have arrived at the solution to Love's "problem" mentioned above—the ability of Love to create another— this creation of another allowing Love to express its true nature as Love—while also allowing Love to maintain its infinite singularity in eternal, united, limitless giving and receiving. As Hafiz says:

دلت به وصل گل ای بلبل سحر خوش باد
که در چمن همه گلبانگ عاشقانهء توست

O ightingale ɔf
the norning

rejoice for your
heart has become
united with
the rose
and all of the
love songs in
the meadow
are now yours.

As there is no end to the giving of Love so too there
is no end to Love's creativity:

حسن بی پایان او و چندان که عاشق میکشد
زمرهیی دیگر به عشق از غیب سر بر میکنند

No matter
how many lovers
His limitless
beauty kills
another group
in love
will raise
their heads
from the unseen.

Or:

بگرفت کار حسنت چون عشق من کمالی
خوش باش از آنکه نبود این هر دو را زوالی

Your beauty
like my
love has
become
perfect
fortunately
neither will ever
decline.

Or:

ماجرای من و معشوق مرا پایان نیست
هرچه آغاز ندارد نپذیرد انجام

As this affair
between me
and my Beloved
has no beginning
so too it has
no end.

Or again:

مدار نقطهء بینش ز خال توست مرا
که قدر گوهر یکدانه گوهری داند

The orbit of
sight of
the pupil of
my eye is
the beauty mark
on your cheek
the value of
a priceless pearl
only a pearl
knows.

BEAUTY IN DANTE'S *DIVINE COMEDY*

Franco Masciandaro

> In everything which gives us the pure authentic feeling of beauty there is really the presence of God. There is, as it were, an incarnation of God in the world, and it is indicated by beauty. The beautiful is the experimental proof that the incarnation is possible.
>
> – Simone Weil

I

Like the sigh, the gaze, or the smile, beauty is an unfathomable language unto itself. It is experienced at once *before* and *beyond* language, before and beyond discursive reasoning. It is at once immanent and transcendent, belonging to the here and now of our earthly existence and a sign or "incarnation of God," as Simone Weil observed. Hence beauty is also intimately related to the Good, the metaphysical *Summum Bonum*: it is its manifestation or epiphany. As we read in Genesis (I:31and II:1), "God saw all he had made, and indeed it was very good . . . Thus heaven and earth were completed with all their array." And as the Book of Wisdom (XI:21) teaches us, God "ordered all things by measure, number, weight." In the first canto of *Paradiso* (103-105) Beatrice speaks of the same order: "All things, among themselves, / possess an order; and this order is / the form that makes the universe like God."[1] As Umberto Eco has noted, in medieval times

---

[1] All citations of the *Divine Comedy* in English are from Allen Mandelbaum's *The Divine Comedy of Dante Alighieri*, 3 vols. (Berkeley: University of California Press, 1982).

these concepts were taken to be aesthetic as well as cosmological . . . It was the Scriptures. . . extended and amplified by the Fathers, which produced this pancalistic vision of the cosmos. But it was confirmed also by the Classical heritage. The theory that the beauty of the world is an image and reflection of Ideal Beauty is Platonic in origin. When Chalcidius, in his Commentary on the *Timaeus*, wrote of the world's incomparable beauty, he was echoing the conclusion of a work fundamental in the formation of medieval thought.[2]

In his *Convivio* (*The Banquet*, III.ii.17-18), citing Boethius's *Consolation of Philosophy* (I, 5 and III, meter 9, 6-8), Dante addresses these words to God: "You produce all things from the supernal exemplar, you, most beautiful, bearing in your mind the beautiful world."[3]

The idea of the goodness and beauty of creation as an image and reflection of the goodness and beauty of God constitutes the fundamental principle of *mimesis* that informs Dante's poem. As we read in *Inferno* XI, a similar relationship exists between art and God's creation, as Virgil, citing Aristotle, explains to Dante the wayfarer:

"Philosophy, for one who understands,
points out, and not in just one place," he said,
"how nature follows—as she takes her course—
    the Divine Intellect and Divine Art;
and if you read your *Physics* carefully,
not many pages from the start, you'll see
    that when it can, your art would follow
        nature,

---

[2] Umberto Eco, *Art and Beauty in the Middle Ages*, trans. by Hugh Bredin (New Haven and London: Yale University Press, 1986), 17. See Plato, *Timaeus*, trans. A. E. Taylor (London, 1929), 100.
[3] *Dante's Il Convivio (The Banquet)*, trans. Richard H. Lansing (New York: Garland, 1990), 93.

just as a pupil imitates his master;
so that your art is almost God's grandchild."
(*Inf.* XI.97-105)

As I comment on a selection of scenes from the *Divine Comedy*, I shall pay special attention to the creative function of beauty, including its effect on our experience as readers, in the narrow economy of a scene or episode, but also, as deemed pertinent, within the larger economy of Dante's journey to God and His City inscribed in the entire poem.

II

In *Inferno* I, we find this scene, in which the goodness of God's creation described in *Genesis* is represented as beautiful:
> The time was the beginning of the morning;
> the sun was rising now in fellowship
> with the same stars that had escorted it
> > when Divine Love first moved those things of
> > > beauty;
> so that the hour and the gentle season
> gave me good cause for hopefulness on seeing
> > that beast before me with her gay skin.
(*Inf.* I.37-43)

The preceding scene of the threatening leopardess (31-36), which had blocked the wayfarer's ascent of the hill, whose shoulders were clothed by the rays of the sun, "which serves to lead men straight along all roads" (16-18), is now radically transformed and transcended the moment the protagonist discovers that the temporal frame is the mythical *illud tempus*, the very beginning of time, coinciding with God's creation of the "beautiful things." As he experiences "hopefulness" at the sight of the leopardess, he resembles Adam, who before the Fall, in the Garden of Eden, experienced harmony with all the beautiful things of creation. "Friendship with the wild animals," writes Mircea Eliade, "and their spontaneous acceptance of men's

15

authority are manifest signs of the recovery of the paradisiac situation."[4] The wayfarer's "return" to or nostalgia for Eden soon proves to be illusory as it clashes with the reaffirmation of an insurmountable evil, manifested this time by the appearance of a terrifying lion and, finally, by a ravenous she-wolf that thrusts him back to the dark wood "where the sun is silent" (*Inf.* I.60). As he discovers the propitious confluence in his time of the mythic time of creation, and acts as if he had suddenly attained the Earthly Paradise, he fails to see that he is still outside the "garden," that he is on a "desert slope" (I.29), which soon the poet will define as a "vast desert ("gran diserto" I.64), where the wayfarer will encounter the soul of Virgil.

I should mention that in the scene of the "vast desert" the poet portrays first the wayfarer's encounter with an unknown Other, to whom he addresses words—"*Miserere di me . . . qual che tu sii*" ("have pity on me . . . whatever you may be" *Inf.* I.65-66)— that echo the words of the most famous of the Penitential Psalms (number 50 of the Vulgate), which are addressed by the psalmist to God: "Miserere mei Deus" ("Have mercy on me, O God"). Thus, this unknown Other appears to the wayfarer first as a *figura Dei* (a figure of God), before he identifies himself as Virgil. After Virgil has revealed his identity (I.67-75), asking, "But why do you return to wretchedness? / Why not climb up the mountain of delight, / the origin and cause of every joy?" (I.76-78), Dante the wayfarer addresses him with these words:

> "And are you then that Virgil, you the
>   fountain
> that freely pours so rich a stream of speech?"
> I answered him with shame upon my brow.
>   "O light and honor of all other poets,
> may my long study and intense love
> that made me search your volume serve me now.

---

[4] Mircea Eliade, *Myths, Dreams and Mysteries*, trans. Philip Mairet (New York: Harper & Row, 1967), 68.

You are my master and my author, you—
the only one from whom my writing drew
the beautiful style for which I have been
   honored.
   You see the beast that made me turn aside;
help me, o famous sage, to stand against her,
for she has made my blood and pulses shudder.
   (*Inf.* I.79-90)[5]

As we focus on the wayfarer's words "lo bello stile" ("the beautiful style"), we must note that they possess a special force, for they reassert, in synthesis, what has characterized the scene we have previously studied: the power of poetry as pure form, as a unique manifestation of beauty, and hence of poetry that can be quite alluring to the wayfarer-poet, as alluring as the "lonza" (the "leopardess') with the attractive "gay skin" has earlier been to him after he had just emerged from the dark wood. As soon as the wayfarer recognizes Virgil in terms of his "stream of speech" and "beautiful style," that is, as soon as he has internalized this "figure" or this "mask" of the poet Virgil, linking it to his own experience as poet, a contrasting assertion emerges, and with it the possibility to construct a new scene. This new assertion begins with the wayfarer's definition of Virgil as "famous sage," a definition that, significantly, is directly proportional to the new definition of the scene, which is now unmistakably one in which the she-wolf is again in focus as a dominant, real presence. In this moment of awakened attention to the dramatic ratio of agent-scene-action, both the wayfarer and Virgil (as well as the reader) know that no "stream of speech" or "beautiful style," no "flight" to Parnassus or nostalgia for Eden, can, *by itself,* exorcise this presence, this manifestation of the irreducible fact of evil.[6] There is nothing ambiguous about this beast.

---

[5] Mandelbaum's translation of Dante's "bello stile" as "noble style" fails to render the full meaning of the original Italian words: "beautiful style."
[6] A similar interpretation has been proposed by Rachel Jacoff and William A. Stephany in *Lectura Dantis Americana: Inferno II*

She does not have the beautiful coat, the "gay skin" of the "lonza" which could stir the aesthetic sensibility of the wayfarer-poet, luring him into the illusion that Eden-Parnassus was within reach.[7] The she-wolf's presence is felt in the very fibers of the wayfarer's being; she makes his "blood and pulses shudder." This is much more than a mere image that appears to the mind's eye and kindles the imagination. She is *there, now.* Her presence permits no escape toward the sunlit "mountain of delight." The one whose help the wayfarer had earlier invoked with the words "*Miserere di me*" is—appropriately to this scene of terror and anguish, marked by the absolute fear of death—the one who, "re-entering" the scene as both poet and sage, points to another scene, another journey:

> "It is another path that you must take,"
> he answered when he saw my tearfulness,
> "if you would leave this savage wilderness;
>   the beast that is the cause of your outcry
> allows no man to pass along her track,
> but blocks him even to the point of death

(Philadelphia: University of Pennsylvania Press, 1989). Commenting on *Inferno* I.82-87, they write: "Dante's hope that his long study and great love for Virgil's poem would somehow deliver him from his spiritual wilderness is touching and moving, but it is also, in terms of a rhetoric of conversion, patently vain: philology and literary affiliation may be important human activities, but they cannot on their own terms fill Dante's spiritual void. His praise of Virgil as the sole source of his own honor as a poet shows in retrospect how imperfectly he understands at the poem's beginning what he will come to learn during its course: the true nature of honor and of poetry, as well as the transformed role Virgil will come to play in his life and his writing" (72). I should add that, correspondingly, during the course of the poem the "bello stile" or beauty of Dante's poetry and of art in general will reveal new, unexpected depths in meaning as a creative force.
[7] Cf. *Purgatorio* XXVIII.139-144, where, in the Earthly Paradise, Matelda tells Dante, Virgil, and Statius: "Those ancients who in poetry presented / the golden age, who sang its happy state, / perhaps, in their Parnassus, dreamt this place."

. . .

> I think and judge it best for you
> to follow me, and I shall guide you, taking
> you from this place through an eternal place,
>   where you shall hear the howls of desperation

. . .

>   and you shall see those souls who are content
> within the fire, for they hope to reach—
> whenever that may be—the blessed people.
>   If you would then ascend as high as these,
> a soul more worthy than I am will guide you;
> I'll leave you in her care when I depart."
>   (*Inf.* I.91-96; 112-115; 118-123)

We should note that if Dante the wayfarer's "return" to the state of innocence of the Earthly Paradise, represented in the *Commedia*'s prologue scene, proves to be illusory, it also reveals the power of beauty, expressed mainly by light, to kindle his desire to attain the state of innocence and happiness analogous to the state experienced by Adam and Eve in Eden before the Fall. This desire will be fulfilled when—after having encountered a plurality of forms of evil in his journey through Hell, and of expiation of evil on the Mountain of Purgatory—he will enter, at the summit of this mountain, the Earthly Paradise. This experience prepares him for his ascent through the heavens, which will end with his vision of God. We must include the beauty-as-light as an attribute of the worthiness as poet, as Dante the wayfarer had attributed to Virgil, addressing him with the words "O light and honor of all other poets" (I.70). The beauty-as-light that we have encountered in the *Commedia*'s first canto foreshadows the fundamental role that it plays throughout the entire poem, especially in *Paradiso*. As Joseph Mazzeo explains,

> The *Divine Comedy* is, from one point of view, an anatomy of love . . . It is also an anatomy of beauty, beauty which takes as many analogous and corresponding forms as there are loves. The universe of the poem is finally entirely reduced in

the *Paradiso* to the interplay of love and beauty, beauty which . . . is primarily manifested *as* light and *through* vision. The two—love and beauty as light—constitute the very structure of the universe and do so functionally: they are not merely architectural elements but the basic concepts in terms of which the poem is articulated and through which it conveys its meaning. They make the journey possible and determine its nature.[8]

We should also note that, especially in *Paradiso*, we find numerous examples of the idea of   beauty-as-light reflecting Thomas Aquinas's definition of *claritas*, as an attribute of beauty (the others being integrity or perfection, and due proportion or consonance; *Summa Theol.* Ia, q. 39, a. 8). As Umberto Eco has noted, "*Claritas* is the one principle of expressiveness in medieval times which could fill the place occupied nowadays by such concepts as the lyricism or symbolism or iconicity of form."[9]

III

In *Inferno* IV we encounter the following scene, which is strikingly informed by the poetics of beauty-as-light, or as *claritas*:

> And so I saw that splendid school assembled,
> led by the lord of song incomparable,
> who like an eagle soars above the rest.
>   Soon after they had talked awhile together,
> they turned to me, saluting cordially
> and having witnessed this, my master smiled;
>   and even greater honor then was mine,
> for they invited me to join their ranks—
> I was the sixth among such wisdom.

---

[8] Joseph Anthony Mazzeo, *Structure and Thought in the "Paradiso"* (Ithaca, NY: Cornell University Press, 1982), 1-2.
[9] Eco, *Art and Beauty*, 81.

So did we move along and toward the light,
talking of things about which silence here
is just as seemly as our speech was there.
We reached the base of an exalted castle,
encircled seven times by towering walls,
defended all around by a fair stream.
We forded this as if upon hard ground;
I entered seven portals with these sages;
we reached a meadow of green flowering plants
. . .
We drew aside to one part of the meadow,
an open place both high and filled with light,
and we could see all those who were assembled.

(Inf. IV.94-111; 115-117)[10]

The "splendid school' ("la bella scuola") is the assembly of
the ancient poets led by Homer. The ritual of honoring
Virgil, represented before the present scene (IV.80-81), is
now extended to Dante, "making him sixth among such
wisdom." As we pause to find meaning in the scene-action
relationship unfolding before our eyes, we are struck by the
presence of distinctive elements of the *topos* of the *locus
amoenus* (i.e., "beautiful place," or "the place that is a
delight to behold"): the beautiful stream ("bel fiumicello"),
the "meadow of green flowering plants," and the luminous
high place within the walls of the castle. They speak of the
paradisal state, but also, because of the pre-eminence given
here to the poets, of a kind of Parnassus. Moreover, the
contiguity of the castle and the garden may represent
humanity's attempt to reconcile the forces of nature and of
art, and thus to recapture the lost pristine order and beauty
of the mythical Golden Age sung by the ancient poets. For
our Christian poet this would constitute a partial recovery
of the original harmony existing between humankind and
nature, between work or art and the forces of nature, as we

---

[10] We should note that Mandelbaum translates the original
expression "bella scuola" (literally, "beautiful school") with the
words "splendid school", and "bel fiumicello" (literally,
"beautiful stream") with the words "fair stream."

find expressed in Genesis 2:15-16: "Yahweh God took the man and settled him in the garden of Eden to cultivate and take care of it." Another important feature of this episode is the fact that the poets cross the beautiful stream surrounding the castle as if it were solid ground ("come terra dura"). This scene seems to echo the Israelites' crossing of the Red Sea, as we read in Exodus 14:22: "The waters parted and the sons of Israel went on dry ground right into the sea." As he enters the noble castle, in the company of the ancient poets, Dante the wayfarer is experiencing, at least in part, a kind of return to Eden, and thus a measure of recapturing what had been denied him by the threatening presence of the three beasts in the Prologue scene and therefore by the reality of sin and evil.

Having commented on the creative power of beauty-as-light of this episode, we should also note that it necessarily expresses the beauty of Dante's poetry, of his art or craft. And we should also find remarkable these words of the poet that we have cited: "So did we move along and toward the light, / talking of things about which silence here / is just as seemly as our speech was there" ("parlando cose che 'l tacere è bello"). Yes, the beauty of the unspoken words, that at once confirm and transcend the beauty of spoken words. I am reminded of these famous verses from "An Ode on a Grecian Urn" by John Keats: "Heard melodies are sweet, but those unheard are sweeter."

IV

The glory of the One who moves all things
permeates the universe but glows
in one part more and in another less.
I was within the heaven that receives
more of His light; and I saw things that he
who from that height descends, forgets or can
not speak; for nearing its desired end,
our intellect sinks into an abyss
so deep that memory fails to follow it.
Nevertheless, as much as I, within

my mind, could treasure of the holy kingdom
shall now become the matter of my song.

(Par. I.1-12)

In sharp contrast with the opening verses of *Inferno* I
("When I had journeyed half of our life's way / I found
myself within a shadowed forest"), and of *Purgatorio* I ("To
course across more kindly waters now / my talent's little
vessel lifts her sails"), which evoke the human condition of
the *nunc fluens* of the "river of time," here the poet—
appropriately, since he is introducing his experience in
Paradise and, correspondingly, the third *cantica* named
Paradiso— speaks of the *nunc stans*, of the timeless eternal
now of the presence in the universe of God the Prime
Mover, expressed by His glory, that is, His light or splendor,
and hence His beauty. In his *Letter to Can Grande* (*Epist.*
XIII.64-65) Dante wrote this commentary: "It is therefore
well said when it says that the divine ray, or divine glory
pierces and reglows through the universe. It pierces as to
essence; it reglows as to being." In his *Convivio* (III.xiv.4)
Dante wrote: "We are further to know that the prime
agent—to wit God—stamps his power upon some things
after the manner of a direct ray, and upon others after the
manner of a reflected splendor; for upon the intelligences
[i.e., the angels] the divine light rays without medium,
upon other things it is reflected by those intelligences which
are first enlightened."

It is important to note that at the beginning of
Paradiso the poet speaks of his ineffable experience, at the
end of his journey, in the transcendent Empyrean—the
"Heaven that receives more of [God's] light." Thus, as the
poet suggests, he is saying something analogous to T. S.
Eliot's words, "In my end is my beginning" (*Four Quartets*,
"East Coker," V.209). This beginning is marked by the
topos of ineffability, which the poet introduces with his
neologism *trasumanar*, one of many that are, significantly,
prevalent in *Paradiso*. The original verse, "Trasumanar
significar *per verba*," can only be inadequately translated:

Passing beyond the human cannot be

worded; let Glaucus serve as simile—
until grace grant you the experience.
    Whether I only was the part of me
That You created last, You—governing
the heavens—know: it was your light that raised me.
    When that wheel which You make eternal
        through
the heavens' longing for You drew me with
the harmony You temper and distinguish,
    the fire of the sun then seemed to me
to kindle so much of the sky, that rain
or river never formed so broad a lake.
    The newness of the sound and the great light
incited me to learn their cause—I was
more keen than I had ever been before.
                    (*Par.* I.70-84)

As the poet acknowledges the ineffability of the extraordinary experience of his vision of God, face to face, preceded by his vision of the heavens—beginning with the Heaven of the Moon—where he will encounter many blessed souls, he nevertheless finds the words, such as *trasumanar*, which he coins, including, as we are discovering again and again, his images of light, whereby he expresses the "truth" of his fiction, that is, the paradox that it is not a fiction. The same can be said of the beauty of his art, often marked by the beauty-as-light. These remarks by Hans-Georg Gadamer, in his essay *The Relevance of the Beautiful*, are a fine illustration of the paradox of the truth of the beauty of art: "In the beautiful presented in nature and art, we experience this convincing illumination of truth and harmony, which compels the admission: 'This is true.' ... The ontological function of the beautiful is to bridge the chasm between the ideal and the real."[11] We should note that Dante bridges the chasm between the ideal and the real, invoking the "example" (the *essemplo* of the original)—

---

[11] Hans-Georg Gadamer, *The Relevance of the Beautiful and Other Essays*, trans. Nicholas Walker, ed. Robert Bernasconi (Cambridge: Cambridge University Press, 1986), 15.

notably, a fiction—of Glaucus becoming immortal like a
god, as we read in Ovid's *Metamorphoses* (XIII.904-59).
Another example which he evokes, but which is not a
fiction, are St. Paul's words expressing his experience (2
Cor. XII:3-4): "I do know. . . that this same person—
whether in the body or out of the body, I do not know; God
knows—was caught up into paradise and heard things
which must not and cannot be put into human language."
Here is Dante's recollection of his ascent to Paradise:

> Whether I only was the part of me
> that You created last, You—governing
> the heavens—know: it was Your light that raised me.
> (*Par.* I.73-75)

As we compare these words with St. Paul's words, we
experience the power of Dante's imitation of this
"example," whereby he at once expresses the ineffability of
the saint's spiritual experience of his mystical vision and
transcends it by the use of his poetics of beauty-as-light,
which makes visible the metaphysics of light, as he
addresses God, saying "It was Your light that raised me."

Dante then recalls his wonderment as he felt drawn to
the harmony of the spheres as well as to the intense light of
the sun, addressing God with these words:

> When that wheel which You make eternal
>   through
> the heavens' longing for You drew me with
> the harmony You temper and distinguish,
>   the fire of the sun then seemed to me
> to kindle so much of the sky, that rain
> or river never formed so broad a lake.
>   The newness of the sound and the great light
> incited me to learn their cause—I was
> more keen than I had ever been before.
> (*Par.*I.76-84)

We should note that here the beauty of Dante's craft is
expressed by his representation of both the beauty of the

music of the spheres and the beauty of the sun's intense light. Such beauty engenders in the wayfarer wonder, which "incites' him "to learn their cause." As Plato and Aristotle taught us, wonder, *thaumázein,* is the origin of knowledge, of philosophy.[12]

Beatrice, who read Dante's mind, explains to him the reason, or cause, of his present extraordinary experience of being drawn toward the intense light of the sun, revealing to him that he is no longer in the Earthly Paradise, but with her is flying toward the Empyrean, the final goal of his journey, when he will see God face to face:

> "The Providence that has arrayed all this
> forever quiets—with Its light—that heaven
> in which the swiftest of the spheres revolves;
>> to there, as toward a destined place, we now
> are carried by the power of the bow
> that always aims its shaft at a glad mark
> . . .
>> You should—if I am right—
> not feel more marvel at your climbing than
> you would were you considering a stream
> that from a mountain's height falls to its base.
> It would be cause for wonder in you if,
> no longer hindered, you remained below,
> as if, on earth, a living flame stood still."
> Then she again turned her gaze heavenward.
> (*Par.* I.121-126; 136-142)

Again, we witness the creativity, indeed the beauty of Dante's poetics of light, of *claritas,* whereby he renders visible, in human, familiar terms, with the image of the "living flame," the metaphysics of light, as he interprets the love of all of creation, including the heavenly spheres, to be united with the Creator's love and His light, in the

---

[12] Plato, *Theaetetus* 155d: "Socrates: This sense of wonder is the mark of the philosopher. Philosophy indeed has no other origin." Aristotle, *Metaphysics* 982b11: "It is because of wonder that men both now and formerly began to philosophize."

transcendent Empyrean, in which, as we read "the swiftest of the spheres revolves," that is, the Primum Mobile. Charles S. Singleton has written this illuminating gloss:

> The final verse of the *Purgatorio* gives us the pilgrim as being "puro e disposto a salire alle stelle" ["pure and prepared to climb unto the stars"], that is, without any remaining impediment in the proper upward direction of his love. His love of choice is now in perfect harmony with his natural love, which has its natural gravitation toward God . . . The upward journey of the pilgrim . . . reflects a *possible* journey of "whichever" living man is uplifted in desire and contemplation toward God: the natural gravitation of God-given love. But love is better symbolized by fire than by water; so Beatrice again returns to fire, to conclude her discourse. If one were to see a flame that does not reach up (toward its proper place above), this quietness would be a marvel as great as the upward flow of a river. But the flame has within it a natural love which seeks to rise. Even so the human heart."[13]

V

In the second canto of *Paradiso* Dante continues to elaborate his poetics of the beauty of light, of *claritas,* as we find in these verses:

> The thirst that is innate and everlasting—
> thirst for the godly realm—bore us away
> as swiftly as the heavens that you see.
> Beatrice gazed upward. I watched her.
> But in a span perhaps no longer than

---

[13] Dante Alighieri, *Paradiso,* trans. with commentary by Charles S. Singleton (Princeton, NJ: Princeton University Press, 1977), 35-36.

an arrow takes to strike, to fly, to leave
    the bow, I reached a place where I could see
that something wonderful drew me; and she
from whom my need could not be hidden, turned
    to me (her gladness matched her loveliness):
"Direct your mind to God in gratefulness,"
she said; "He has brought us to the first star."
    It seemed to me that we were covered by
a brilliant, solid, dense, and stainless cloud,
and much like a diamond that the sun has struck.
    Into itself the everlasting pearl
received us, just as water will accept
a ray of light and yet remain intact.
    If I was body (and on earth we can
not see how things material can share
one space—the case when body enters body),
    than should our longing be still more inflamed
to see that Essence in which we discern
how God and human nature were made one.
                         (Par. II.19-42)

Once again, we witness and are moved by the creative power of Dante's poetry, by its beauty expressed by images of light, implicitly by its multiform beauty—such as that of the moon as a diaphanous "stainless cloud" resembling a diamond struck by the sun, and as a pearl that, in turn, resembles the brightness of water traversed by a "ray of light." Correspondingly, this scene, marked by the beauty of light, is enlivened by the image of Beatrice's gladness that matches her beauty (being "sì lieta come bella"). Equally remarkable is the new experience of the pilgrim's *trasumanar*, which, analogous to the state of the blessed souls, is manifested by the beauty of light. As the poet tells us, if he, like St. Paul, knows not if with or without his body, he nevertheless has become like a "ray of light" that traverses water, thus resembling the glorified luminosity of the blessed souls.

VI

We find other examples of this splendor, or *claritas*, in the
third canto of *Paradiso*, in which Dante represents, in the
sphere of the moon, his encounter with the souls who, like
the moon, were inconstant. Out of the chorus of the blessed
souls emerges Piccarda, a nun who was forced by her
brother, Corso Donati, to marry. She was inconstant, as it
is suggested, for not fulfilling her vows by not attempting to
return to her convent. Nevertheless, as she explains to
Dante, as she appears in the lowest celestial sphere,
indicating the degree of her blessedness, she resides in the
Empyrean, and is not envious of the higher degree of
blessedness of the other souls. As Dante wrote in his
Convivio (III.xv.10), "And this is why the saints envy not
one another, because each one attains the goal of his
longing, which is commensurate with the nature of his
excellence." As we turn our attention to the text, we see how
the poet makes these concepts visible, as he continues to
elaborate his poetics of beauty-as-light:

> Just as, returning through transparent, clean
> glass, or through waters calm and crystalline
> (so shallow that they scarcely can reflect),
>   the mirrored image of our faces meets
> our pupils with no greater force than that
> a pearl has when displayed on a white forehead—
>   so faint, the many faces I saw keen
> to speak . . .
>
> (*Par.* III.10-17)

The images evoked here by the poet emphasize the faintness
of the light that defines the figures   of the blessed souls,
reflecting, appropriately, we can say, the low degree of their
saintliness. Thus, I am reminded of the "due proportion or
consonance" as an attribute of beauty defined by Thomas
Aquinas (as we mentioned earlier). As we think of *claritas*,
we note that here it is expressed not by intense light, or
radiance, but, again appropriately, by the subtle degree of

light, as that of the faint image of our faces reflected in "clean glass" or in "shallow," "crystalline" waters, resembling the fine, almost imperceptible degree of difference between the white of a pearl and the white of a woman's forehead. I am reminded of a painting I saw many years ago, at the New York Museum of Modern Art, by Kazimir Malevich, titled "White on White." Against the background of a square, white canvas, the artist has painted a smaller square, also white, but faintly distinguished from the larger square by its slight difference in hue. Somehow, the almost infinitesimal difference, as well as the likeness, defining the relationship between the two squares, is pleasing to the eye, is therefore beautiful. I recall these reflections on the essence of the beautiful by Gadamer, who cites Plato (*Phaedrus* 250d): "Plato describes the beautiful as that which shines forth most clearly and draws us to itself, as the very visibility of the ideal."[14]

As we return to the text, we learn from Beatrice's words addressed to the pilgrim that the souls of the inconstant will speak to him truthfully because they are guided by God's "truthful light":

"... Speak and listen; trust what they say:
the truthful light in which they find their peace
will not allow their steps to turn astray."
(*Par.* III.31-33)

Thus we discern the deep connection between the faint light that defines the souls of the inconstant and God's light—a connection that is further expressed by the following scene of Dante's interaction with Piccarda:

Then I turned to the shade that seemed most anxious
to speak, and I began as would a man
bewildered by desire too intense:
"O spirit born to goodness, you who feel,
beneath the rays of eternal life,

---

[14] Gadamer, *Relevance of the Beautiful*, 15.

that sweetness which cannot be known unless
    it is experienced, it would be gracious
of you to let me know your name and fate."
At this, unhesitant, with smiling eyes:
    "Our charity will never lock its gates
against just will: our love is like the Love
that would have all Its court be like Itself.

    Within the world I was a nun, a virgin;
and if your mind attends and recollects,
my greater beauty here will not conceal me,

    and you will recognize me as Piccarda,
who, placed here with the other blessed ones,
am blessed within the slowest of the spheres.

    Our sentiments, which only serve the flame
that is the pleasure of the Holy Ghost,
delight in their conforming to His order.

    And we are to be found within a sphere
this low, because we have neglected vows,
so that in some respect we were deficient."

    And I to her: "Within your wonderful
semblance there is something divine that glows,
transforming the appearance you once showed:

    therefore, my recognizing you was slow. . ."
                                    (*Par.* III.34-61)

We now experience the richness of Dante's poetics of
beauty-as-light, as he elaborates, and in a sense, perfects the
beauty announced, at the beginning of the episode, by the
faint images of the shadowy souls. The poet now represents
at once the lesser light that defines the state of the blessed
souls of the inconstant and how this light is also a
manifestation of the totally transcendent Light of God, as
we find expressed by the pilgrim's words addressed to
Piccarda about her feeling the "sweetness" of the "rays of
eternal life," and about her "wonderful semblance"
revealing "something divine that glows," as well as by her
declaration of her love being like God's Love, serving "the
flame / that is the pleasure of the Holy Ghost," and by her
speaking of her present "greater beauty," compared to her
beauty on earth, which will not "conceal" her identity.

Hence, we acknowledge and are moved by the beauty of Dante's art, as it fashions the scenes of his encounter with the blessed souls in the sphere of the Moon, representing at once the low degree of their paradisal state and their experiencing the "sweetness" of "the rays of the eternal life," like the white pearl that is at once distinct and like the "white forehead," or like the smaller white square that it stands out, thought faintly, against the background of the larger white square of the painting "White on White."

VII

The scenes of the pilgrim's ascent into Venus and of the souls clothed in light, who like "wheeling lamps" descend from the Empyrean to greet him and Beatrice, constitute the creative platform for the representation of Dante's encounter with his friend, Charles Martel (son of Charles II of Anjou and Mary of Hungary), and thus the celebration of the beauty of friendship:

> I did not notice my ascent to it,
> yet I was sure I was in Venus when
> I saw my lady grow more beautiful.
> And just as, in a flame, a spark is seen,
> and as, in plainsong, voice in voice is heard—
> one holds the note, the other comes and goes—
> I saw in that light other wheeling lamps,
> some more and some less swift, yet in accord,
> I think, with what their inner vision was.
>
> (*Par.* VIII.13-21)

As Dante evokes his entrance into Venus, his is the language of love, of intimacy and communion, as exemplified by a spark within a flame and by a voice heard within another voice, which does not obliterate difference as it reveals the union of two distinct bodies and two distinct natures. It is also the language of self-surrender, of the I that becomes a subject whose self-awareness and the awareness of the new reality that surrounds him is dependent on the other, the beloved: the pilgrim's experience of entering the luminous planet Venus remains hidden, secret, and as mysterious and unfathomable as the moment of discovering himself in Venus by virtue of the beloved's equally mysterious and unfathomable heightened beauty.

As we focus on the pilgrim's vision of the approaching souls, we note that it is rendered through images of light, of *claritas,* and hence of beauty, that continue to make visible the idea of communion and corresponding harmony that is born of and celebrates difference, as manifested by the more or less swiftness of the "wheeling lamps."

When the "circling dance" of the spirits comes to a halt, and after they welcome the pilgrim, singing "*Hosanna*"—thus echoing the cry of *Hosanna* addressed to Jesus as he entered Jerusalem (Matt. 21:9)—one of them emerges from this "chorus" to greet the pilgrim:

> Then one drew near us, and began
> alone: "We all are ready at your pleasure,
> so that you may receive delight from us.
>   One circle and one circling and one thirst
> are ours as we revolve with the celestial
> Princes whom, from the world, you once invoked:
>   '*You who, through understanding move the
>   third
> Heaven.*' Our love is so complete—to bring
> you joy, brief respite will not be less sweet."
>   (*Par.* VIII.31-39)

As we witness this scene along with the pilgrim, we note that the soul who addresses him, before revealing his identity as Dante's friend, speaks at once as one and in the name of the chorus of the blessed souls who with him revolve in perfect harmony with the angels who move the planet Venus, sharing with them their vision of God and their unending thirst to be in communion with Him. While remaining hidden, this spirit begins to hint at his special relation with the pilgrim by citing his poem, *You who, through understanding, move the third heaven* (the first *canzone* of Dante's *Convivio*). Thus, as the unknown other, a stranger from the pilgrim's (and the reader's) perspective, he speaks with the familiarity of friendship. And he declares his love as well as the love of the other spirits for the pilgrim by expressing his and their desire to bring him joy, momentarily interrupting his and their "circling" in order to engage in conversation with him. To this unrecognized spirit, who has shown signs of friendship, the pilgrim addresses these words, after receiving his lady's consent:

> . . . "Tell me, who are you?" I asked
> in a voice stamped with loving sentiment.
>   And how much larger, brighter did I see
> that spirit grow when, as I spoke, it felt
> the new joy that was added to its joys!
> (Par. VIII.44-48)

We recognize the power of the word, and of the *voice* that here is "di grande affetto impressa" (stamped with great affection), whereby the pilgrim expresses his love of one who is still a stranger. As we observe with the pilgrim the spirit's enlarged joy, expressed by its increased brightness, upon hearing the pilgrim's affectionate words, we are reminded of a similar demonstration of the love that the blessed share with God's Infinite Love when "a thousand splendors," as they appeared to Dante in the Heaven of Mercury, "each declared: / Here now is one who will increase our loves" (*Par.* V.103-105).

The expansion of love kindled by the pilgrim's words and by his voice increases as the joyful spirit reveals his identity without mentioning his name:

> Thus changed, he then replied: "The world
>   held me
> briefly below; but had my stay been longer,
> much evil that will be, would not have been.
>   My happiness, surrounding me with rays,
> keeps me concealed from you; it hides me like
> a creature that swathed in its own silk.
>   You loved me much and had good cause for
>   that;

for had I stayed below, I should have showed
you more of my love than the leaves alone."
(Par. VIII.49-57)

Contrary to what the reader might expect, Charles begins
to identify himself as Dante's friend by focusing on the evil
that "would not have been" had he lived longer (he died at
the age of twenty-four, one year after meeting Dante in
Florence), *before* mentioning the love that still binds him to
Dante. Thus, as the text suggests, their friendship is of the
highest order, for it is not only based on familiarity and on
their shared delight in philosophical poetry, as shown by
Charles' recollection of Dante's *canzone*, but is also based
on worthiness and on their shared disinterested love of the
good. Equally notable is Charles' declaration to his friend
that the very happiness that he now experiences, as he and
Dante are reunited, causes his physical identity to be
concealed by the light that manifests such happiness—a
light that, as we have noted, has become brighter as Dante
spoke words "in a voice stamped with loving sentiment."
Hence a new identity emerges that transcends Charles'
earthly identity, revealing by virtue of his brightness the
degree of his communion with God's Infinite Love. This
brightness, and hence its beauty, we may now say, is
analogous to Beatrice's heightened beauty, which signaled
to the pilgrim his ascent to Venus.

VIII

Mindful of "lo fren de l'arte" ("the curb of art"), of which
our poet wrote before ending *Purgatorio,* I shall now bring
my commentary to a close, focusing on the thirtieth canto
of *Paradiso,* in which Dante celebrates the beauty of
Beatrice and, correspondingly, the beauty of the Empyrean.
We shall now discover anew the beauty of Dante's poetry as
it fashions scenes embodying the beauty of light, of *claritas,*
that at once recalls and transcends human experience, the
trasumanar announced by the poet at the beginning of
Paradiso:

If that which has been said of her so far
were all contained within a single praise,
it would be much too scant to serve me now.
　　The loveliness I saw surpassed not only
our human measure—and I think that, surely,
only its Maker can enjoy it fully
. . .
　　Like the sun that strikes the frailest eyes,
so does the memory of her sweet smile
deprive me of the use of my own mind.
　　From that first day when, in this life, I saw
her face, until I had this vision, no
thing ever cut the sequence of my song,
　　but now I must desist from this pursuit,
in verses, of her loveliness, just as
each artist who has reached his limit must.
　　So she, in beauty (as I leave her to
a herald that is greater than my trumpet,
which nears the end of its hard theme), with voice
　　and bearing of a guide whose work is done,
began again: "From matter's largest sphere,
we now have reached the heaven of pure light,
　　light of the intellect, light filled with love,
love of true good, love filled with happiness,
a happiness surpassing every sweetness.
　　Here you will see both ranks of Paradise
and see one of them wearing that same aspect
which you will see again at Judgement Day."
　　　　　　　　　　　　　　　(*Par.* XXX.16-21; 25-45)

As the poet experiences a higher degree of his failure to
adequately represent Beatrice's beauty, paradoxically, he
gives new expression to the *topos* of ineffability, once again
by relying on images of light, and its beauty, as described by
Beatrice, revealing to Dante that they have now entered the
Empyrean, the "heaven of pure light": light of the intellect,
and hence of vision, which the wayfarer shares with the
reader; light filled with love of the good, and love "filled
with happiness," "happiness surpassing every sweetness."
The wonderment we have so far experienced as readers of

the *Commedia*, and thus, ideally, as companions of Dante the wayfarer and Dante the poet, is now at once relived and "surpassed," transcended, especially as we read of Beatrice announcing that to the pilgrim will be granted the extraordinary vision of the glorified bodies of the blessed on Judgment Day. As Charles Singleton explains,

> By a very special privilege the wayfarer, a living man who has attained to this ultimate goal, is to be shown the human souls of the elect as they will be seen after the Last Judgment, when they will have their bodies (glorified bodies) again. Here the poet is quite on his own, for no accepted doctrine concerning the attainment of this pinnacle of contemplation on the part of a living man allows any such privilege. But now the poet allows it and crowns his poem with such embodied vision (by special privilege), thus climaxing the whole structure with the kind of vision which is the very substance of his poetry . . . Human souls that have been flames, without human countenance or bodily semblance throughout most of *Paradiso*, are now to be seen in their glorified bodies.[15]

We recall that, in *Paradiso* XIV—another fine example of Dante's poetics of beauty-as-light—the wayfarer learned the following from the "light" of Salomon, in the sphere of the Sun:

> "As long as the festivity
> of Paradise shall be, so long shall our
> love radiate around us such a garment.
> Its brightness takes its measure from our ardor,
> our ardor from our vision, which is measured
> by what grace each receives, beyond his merit.
> When, glorified and sanctified, the flesh
> is once again our dress, our persons shall,

---

[15] Singleton, in *Paradiso*, 493.

in being all complete, please all the more;
    therefore, whatever light gratuitous
the Highest Good gives us will be enhanced—
the light that will allow us to see Him;
    that light will cause our vision to increase,
the ardor vision kindles to increase,
the brightness born of ardor to increase.
    Yet even as a coal engenders flame,
but with intenser glow outshines it, so
that in that flame the coal persists, it shows;
    so will the brightness that envelops us
be then surpassed in visibility
by reborn flesh, which earth now covers up . . ."
. . .
    One and the other choir seemed to me
so quick and keen to say "Amen" that they
showed clearly how they longed for their dead
    bodies—
not only for themselves, perhaps, but for
their mothers, fathers, and for others dear
to them before they were eternal flames.
(Par. XIV.37-57; 61-66)

As we return to *Paradiso* XXX, approaching the end of my commentary, I, more than ever, am overwhelmed by the sense of inadequacy, indeed of failure to shed new light (allow me the word play) on Dante's poetics of the beauty of light, of *claritas*. Therefore, I will end with a reading of the following luminous scene, which foreshadows the wayfarer's final vision inscribed in *Paradiso* XXXIII. I shall preface my reading with these words borrowed from Rebecca West's *lectura* of the last canto of *The Divine Comedy*: "The best reading of the last canto of the *Comedy* would perhaps be just that: a reading, out loud, by someone capable of bringing to life the semantic and sonoric splendors of this exquisite finale. How can the words of any commentator, any critic, any teacher, even begin to approach the beauty of these closural lines? I think: let us

read *it*, again, alone, together, silently or aloud . . ."[16] Here
is my reading:

> Come sùbito lampo che discetti
> li spiriti visivi, sì che priva
> da l'atto l'occhio di più forti obietti,
>
> così mi circunfulse luce viva,
> e lasciommi fasciato di tal velo
> del suo fulgor, che nulla m'appariva.
>
> «Sempre l'amor che queta questo cielo
> accoglie in sé con sì fatta salute,
> per far disposto a sua fiamma il candelo».
>
> Non fur più tosto dentro a me venute
> queste parole brievi, ch'io compresi
> me sormontar di sopr' a mia virtute;
>
> e di novella vista mi raccesi
> tale, che nulla luce è tanto mera,
> che li occhi miei non si fosser difesi;
>
> e vidi lume in forma di rivera
> fulvido di fulgore, intra due rive
> dipinte di mirabil primavera.
>
> Di tal fiumana uscian faville vive,
> e d'ogne parte si mettien ne' fiori,
> quasi rubin che oro circunscrive;
>
> poi, come inebrïate da li odori,
> riprofondavan sé nel miro gurge,
> e s'una intrava, un'altra n'uscia fori.
>
> «L'alto disio che mo t'infiamma e urge,
> d'aver notizia di ciò che tu vei,
> tanto mi piace più quanto più turge;

---

[16] Rebecca West, "*Paradiso XXXIII*," in *Dante's* Divine Comedy, *Introductory Readings, III:* Paradiso, ed. Tibor Wlassics, *Special Issue: Lectura Dantis Virginiana, vol. III* (Charlottesville, VA: 1995), 504.

ma di quest' acqua convien che tu bei
prima che tanta sete in te si sazi»:
così mi disse il sol de li occhi miei.
. . .

   e sì come di lei bevve la gronda
de le palpebre mie, così mi parve
di sua lunghezza divenuta tonda.
. . .

   O isplendor di Dio, per cu' io vidi
l'alto trïunfo del regno verace,
dammi virtù a dir com' ïo il vidi!

   Like sudden lightning scattering the spirits
of sight so that the eye is then too weak
to act on other things it would perceive,
   such was the living light encircling me,
leaving me so enveloped by its veil
of radiance that I could see no thing.
   "The Love that calms this heaven always
      welcomes
into Itself with such a salutation,
to make the candle ready for its flame."
   No sooner had these few words entered me
than I became aware that I was rising
beyond the power that was mine; and such
   new vision kindled me again, that even
the purest light would not have been so bright
as to defeat my eyes, deny my sight;
   and I saw light that took a river's form—
light flashing, reddish-gold, between two banks
painted with wonderful spring flowerings.
   Out of that stream there issued living sparks,
which settled on the flowers on all sides,
like rubies set in gold; and then, as if
   intoxicated with the odors, they again
plunged into the amazing flood:
as one spark sank, another spark emerged.
   "The high desire that now inflames, incites,
you to grasp mentally the thing you see,

pleases me more as it swells more; but first,
    that you may satisfy your mighty thirst,
you must drink of these waters." So did she
who is the sun of my eyes speak to me

. . .

    But as my eyelids' eaves drank of that wave,
it seemed to me that it had changed its shape:
no longer straight, that flow now formed a round

. . .

    O radiance of God, through which I saw
the noble triumph of the true realm, give
to me the power to speak of what I saw!
                (*Par.*XXX.46-75; 88-90; 97-99)

BEAUTY

Peter Booth

At the outset, we are dealing with an existence that, in having no substance, is imperceptible. That is, a true vision of God is the awareness that there is nothing that can be seen. For God as Love in His infinite, uncreated state, lacks any form or substance making Him perceptible; and, of course, for the God-Realized soul, there can be no vision at all as vision requires the dialectic of the seer and the seen and this dialectic can only take place when God has brought about the apparent separation of creation. The veils covering God's beauty, then, are actually veils that reveal it and the God-Realized poet is fully aware that his art is an art of manifesting the beauty of God by making the imperceptible perceptible, or, in its highest form, providing a reflection of that which otherwise cannot be perceived. Accordingly, this poetic art is very refined as it may capture a fleeting glimpse of a transcendent being who only occasionally allows Himself to be seen, and certainly this appearance occurs only if the veil manifests some of His limitless beauty, enticing God to dress for a moment in a garb of poetic elegance.

God as Love, in being uncreated, is the only existence, as all else, in being created, experiences the friction of relativity and is ultimately ground down into nothing. The God-Realized poet, in creating veils that partially reflect the Beloved's beauty must have a similar substanceless media to create these manifestations. And for this nothing is better suited than words. Like Love words have no dimension, substance or form; their existence is granted only by the meaning the rational mind ascribes to them. Otherwise they are nothing. Obviously, then, the art of the God-

Realized poet in constructing veils revealing the Beloved's beauty is to take this rationally generated vocabulary, transform it into a vocabulary eclipsing the rational, and enter it into the limitless realms of Love's beauty. This realm is the realm of the heart, as it is in the heart where the purest reflection of God's beauty—where the most subtle veil revealing God's beauty—is found. Hafiz speaks of God's imperceptibility here:

روی تو کس ندید و هزارت رقیب هست
در غنچه یی هنوز و صدت عندلیب هست

No one
has seen
your cheek
despite a
thousand
watching;
although still
in a bud a
hundred
nightingales
sing your
praises.

And he speaks of the limit of the rational mind here:

ای که از دفتر عقل آیت عشق آموزی
ترسم این نکته به تحقیق ندانی دانست

I am
afraid that
bewildered
will remain
the one who
searches in
the book
of reason
for a sign of

the miracle
of love.

Or:

نهادم عقل را ره توشه از می
ز شهر هستی اش کردم روانه

I gave
reason
wine
as a provision
for the road
and sent him
out of
the city
of existence.

As an example of how Hafiz takes a rational
vocabulary and transforms it into a spiritual one —that is,
words as simple objects or concepts into words bordering
on infinity—let's look at two of his most common extended
metaphors—first wine and then a wine goblet or cup:

خرم دل آنکه همچو حافظ
مستی ز می الست گیرد

Joyous is
the heart
that
like Hafiz
is intoxicated
on the
wine of
the covenant
between

God and
man.[1]

Wine then is not so much a symbol of God's existence as infinite Love as it is a symbol for the relationship between God and man, as this is the primary manifestation or expression of Love—that is man himself in being created becomes a veil, or, more specifically, his consciousness becomes a veil:

میان عاشق و معشوق هیچ حایل نیست
تو خود حجاب رهی حافظ از میان بر خیز

Between lover and
Beloved there is no
veil, Hafiz you
yourself are the
veil get out of
the way.[2]

As wine is a relative word for an infinite existence, an entirely new contextual meaning must be formed around it to capture a sense of this infinity. There are many ways to analyze how Hafiz does this, none better than considering

---

[1] روز آلست lit. "the day of the original covenant between God and man" refers to verse 172 in the Koran. آلست : "Am I not your Lord?" "In Persian poetry 'the day of the original covenant between God and man' is the day that man by the divine will and knowledge of God came into existence with his fate written. 'The wine of the covenant between God and man' is the wine of pre-eternity" (Bargnaysi, in حافظ بر اساس نسخه نو یافته بسیر کهن [The Divan of Hafiz (Based on a newly discovered manuscript written around the time of Hafiz)], ed. Sayyed Sadeq Sajjadi and Ali Bahramiyan, with notes and commentary by Kazem Bargnaysi (Tehran: Fekr-e-ruz, 2001), 151. See also Schimmel, *Mystical Dimension of Islam*, 24.

[2] In Islam the veil hiding the effulgence of God is composed of seventy thousand layers of light and darkness. See Annemarie Schimmel, *A Two-Colored Brocade*, 220.

his comparison of a goblet of wine with a tulip blossom as the tulip blossom has the same form as a wine goblet:

مگو که لاله ندانست بی وفایی دهر
که تا بزاد و بشد جام می ز کف ننهاد

> The tulip
> is not
> unaware of
> the faithlessness
> of time
> for from the
> moment of
> its birth
> until the
> time of
> its death
> it never takes
> the wine goblet
> from its
> hand.

Or:

نه این زمان دل حافظ در آتش هوس است
که داغدار ازل همچو لاله خودروست

> It is not
> just in
> this time
> that Hafiz's
> heart is in
> the fire of
> longing like
> the tulip it
> was branded
> with a black
> scar in the

beginning before
time.

The tulip blossom shaped like a wine goblet has a black dot
in the bottom of it, representing the remorse it felt with its
creation as this was accompanied by being separated from
its source. If the tulip's shape is a perfect representation of
the goblet containing the wine symbolizing the intoxication
that both God and man (and presumably the tulip) felt at
the moment of creation, then the black mark in the bottom
of the tulip blossom represents the accompanying sorrow
experienced from the separation that brought it and
everything else into existence. These dual emotions
resulting from the division of God into lover and Beloved—
this division creating the intoxication of Love as well as the
sorrow of separation—form one set of polar opposites of
Hafiz's vast poetic context.

The introduction of this black dot in the bottom of the
tulip accesses another massive metaphoric stream, that of
blackness, indeed sacred blackness, and this Hafiz runs
together with other images of wine and blackness:

چو لاله در قدحم ریز ساقیا می و مشک
که نقش خال نگارم نمیرود ز ضمیر

Saki
pour
fragrant
wine
into my
tulip-like
cup
for the
image
of my
Beloved's
beauty
mark
never goes

from my
heart.[3]

---

[3] ساقی "saki" lit. "the cupbearer," but in Sufi mysticism the pir or
murshid who dispenses the wine of Divine Love. In general, the
saki is the pir or murshid in the form of a young man. Just as
frequently, as he is the spiritual master, he is seen as a wise old
man:

پیر میخانه سحر جام جهان بینم داد
وندر آن آینه از حسن تو کرد آگاهم

At dawn
the master of
the wine tavern
gave me the
world-seeing
cup and in
its reflection
made me
aware of
your beauty.

Kazem Bargnaysi's comments in حافظ بر اساس نسخه نو یافته بسیر کهن
[The Divan of Hafiz] on this couplet apply to the saki as well: "In
the idioms of mysticism, 'the old man of the tavern' (پیر میخانه) is
the 'murshid' (مرشد), the spiritual master, the guide, the 'pivot of
the universe.' جام جهان بین 'the world-seeing cup' is the cup
wherein all of the secrets and the events of the universe are seen.
In the idiom of the sufis, it refers to the heart of the mystic. It is a
heart so pure and resplendent that it displays the beauty of
Reality, the face of the Eternal Beloved and all of the closed secrets
of His creation. In the poetry of Hafiz, the world-seeing cup, and
the cup of wine ("جام می") are completely one and the same, and
in the cup of pure wine he observes the hidden secrets of time.
The cup of wine is brought into being by the loss, the negation
and the freedom from the lower self, which allows the heart to
completely transform itself into the cup of wine. The meaning of
the couplet then is this: 'At the time of dawn the old man of the
tavern gave the cup of wine into my hand and from the possession
of that cup the hidden secrets of creation were mirrored inside of
me and I became aware of the Beloved's beauty.'"

This black spot first mentioned in the tulip and now as the beauty mark on the Beloved's cheek is found throughout Hafiz, with the black beauty mark representing all of creation:

خال مشكين كه بدان عارض گندمگون است
سرّ آن دانه كه شد رهزن آدم با اوست

> The secret of
> the grain that
> brought about
> the fall of Adam
> is with that
> black beauty
> mark on that
> wheatish-colored
> cheek.[4]

These images of blackness and their associations with creation, wine and eventually the water of eternal life stream through Hafiz's poetry in a great confluence expanding the impact of each. At the elevated heights of this development we find Khizer[5], the immortal God-Realized guide of pilgrims and wayfarers. He is said to be the keeper of this water of immortality whose source is a well-spring in the depths of fathomless darkness:

---

[4] "God created Adam in His own image. He projected from Himself that image of His eternal love, that He might behold Himself as in a mirror" (Reynold A. Nicholson, *The Mystics of Islam* [Arkana Penguin Books, 1989], 150)

[5] Khizer resides in the darkest region in creation where the spring of eternal life is believed to exist. "A special relation was constructed between the pen and the Water of Life, as the writer's black ink could easily be compared to the mysterious water that grants immortality and is found only in the darkest depths" (Schimmel, *A Two-Colored Brocade*, 234).

گذار بر ظلمات است خضر راهی کو
مباد کاتش محرومی آب ما ببرد

As our passage
is through the
darkest realm
where Khizer
found the water
of eternal life
where is he
to guide us?
May it not be
that the fire
of privation
carries off
our water
of life.

Before going further it is important to mention
another aspect of Hafiz's style. Rather than his vast
metaphoric streams forming a torrent that rushes to the
ocean—souls returning to the source as it were (as is the
case with many mystical poets)—his streams flow together
to form a pool, or more specifically, to fill a wine goblet.
This imagery, in its vastness and purity, is specifically
designed to reflect the Beloved's beauty:

ما در پیاله عکس رخ یار دیده ایم
ای بیخبر ز لذت شرب مدام ما

You ignorant
ones have
no idea
of the pleasure
our constant
wine drinking
provides for
in our cup
we have seen

the reflection
of the face of
the Friend.

As there can be only one liquid of immortality this
wine of Love is then revealed as Khizer's water of eternal
life:

آبی که خضر حیات ازو یافت
در میکده جو که جام دارد

Seek the
water that
gave
Khizer
eternal life
in the tavern
in a goblet
of wine.

And accordingly, it contains the secrets of existence:

همچو جم جرعهء ما کش که ز سر دو جهان
پرتو جام جهان بین دهدت آگاهی

Just like
king Jamshid
drink our
draught
see the
ray of
light from
our goblet
and
become aware
of the secrets

of both the
worlds.[6]

Returning to our discussion of darkness and
blackness—as in Hafiz before the invisible effulgence of
God, everything is dark or black, even the sun—we find
these metaphoric streams gaining even wider associations
as we have the black pupil of the eye reflecting the black
beauty mark on the Beloved's cheek referring to the black
core of the heart referring to the black spot in the bottom
of a tulip expressing its remorse at the separation it
experienced at the moment of creation—which is what has
happened to everything else that is created—with the tulip
itself representing a goblet of wine, with Khizer's water of
eternal life—also wine—being found in the realm of
greatest darkness, but it is actually there out of shame
before the beauty of Hafiz's poetry:

---

[6] Jamshid: "In the national stories of Iran Jamshid was one of the
greatest kings of the Peshdadian dynasty (the first Dynasty of
Kings in Persia) and the successor to Tahmuras (the third King
in the Peshdadian line and the founder of Babylon, Nineveh and
Isfahan). He invented weapons of war and wine. He is the
founder of the city of Persepolis and the festival of Nou Ruz (the
Persian New Year celebrated on the day of the vernal equinox).
After the Arab invasion and the establishment of Islam in Iran,
the national stories of Iran became mixed with Semitic stories and
Jamshid became likened to Salomon and Alexander, until they
say that when Jamshid's name appeared with the words ring and
signet and horse and throne and wind and fish and birds and the
like then he is being compared to Salomon; and if to a great task,
a mirror, the water of immortality and the like, then the intended
comparison is with Alexander; and if with the wine goblet and
wine and feasts and festivals and Nou Ruz and the like then the
intention is King Jamshid himself. Jamshid's goblet or the world-
revealing goblet that is allied with the name of this king up until
the sixth century was known as the goblet of Kaikhosrou.
Jamshid's goblet or cup in Persian Literature is sometimes related
to the signet ring of Salomon" (Bargnaysi, in
حافظ بر اساس نسخه نو یافته بسیر کهن [The Divan of Hafiz], 608).

حجاب ظلمت از آن بستأب خضر که گشت
ز طبع حافظ و این شعر همچو آب خجل

From shame
before
Hafiz's
natural gifts
and poetry
flowing
like water
Khizer's
water of
eternal life
hid itself
behind a
veil of
darkness.

With the poems describing all of this producing—through words—the pearl of the perfect reflection of God's Being. Hafiz longs to pierce this in "the darkest night," this piercing of the pearl symbolizing union with God's Infinity while being within the extreme darkness of illusion.

وه که دردانه یی چنین نازک
در شب تار سفتنم هوس است

O such a
delicate pearl!
How I long to
pierce it in
the darkest
night![7]

This entire drama being played out in the blackness of the Beloved's curls:

---

[7] For a discussion of the mystical significance of a pearl, see Schimmel, *Mystical Dimension of Islam*, 284.

شبی دل را به تاریکی ز زلفت باز میجستم
رخت میدیدم و جامی هلالی باز میخوردم

One night I
searched for
my heart
in the darkness of
your curls and while
watching your face
I drank from the
wine cup of
the crescent moon.[8]

The heart having been trapped there after failing for the black beauty mark on the Beloved's cheek, with the black ink of Hafiz's pen writing about the whole drama in a way that pours forth the water of life:

آب حیوانش ز منقار بلاعت میچکد
زاغ کلک من بنام ایزد چه عالی مشرب است

In the name
of God how
elevated in nature
is my pen that
the water of life
drips from its
black, crow-like
beak.

Appropriately, as is seen here, it is the poet who reveals the water of immortality that Khizer has hidden in the greatest darkness. That is, it is the poet who manifests or brings to

---

[8] In Persian poetry the face of the Beloved is often compared to the moon. The sliver of the new moon represents the Beloved's eyebrow. This couplet also refers to the belief that seeing the new moon makes one love mad. See Heravi, *A Commentary on the Ghazals of Hafiz*, 200.

light the hidden and the unseen. Here poetry is revelation
creating the language of love and the language of the heart,
as it is the heart that is the goblet of wine and the treasure
house of all of the secrets in creation:

دلم که گوهر اسرار حسن و عشق در وست
توان به دست تو دادن گرش نکو داری

If you take
good care
of it I will
give you
my heart
that contains
the pearl of
the secrets
of love and
beauty.

Or:

دلی که غیب نمای است و جام جم دارد
ز خاتمی که دمی گم شود چه غم دارد

The heart
that reveals
the secrets
and has
the cup of
Jamshid
has nothing
to fear
from having lost
for a moment
the signet ring
of Solomon.

This couplet also being qualification by superlative, as Solomon's ring granting command over all of creation is insignificant before the treasures of the heart.

While we are at it, all of these symbols and images are redemptive in one way or another. The black mark in the bottom of the tulip representing the remorse of separation is redeemed by the shape of the tulip representing a goblet containing the wine of God's Love, and the "black core of the heart" is redeemed by its housing the pearls and gold of spiritual attainment. These elements of redemption are found in all of Hafiz's imagery, and we can see here how Hafiz takes limited rational concepts and through contextual development transforms them into vast extended metaphors bordering on the realm of infinity. These tropes are never stagnant or complete in themselves. Instead they are flowing and open-ended, much like ink flowing from a pen reminding us of the beautiful, vast, extended metaphor throughout Persian mystical poetry of the relationship between the blackness of the realm of the water of immortality and the black ink of the poet's pen.

We can arrive at a similar awareness through completely different but allied set of images. Consider this couplet:

عاقلان نقطهء پرگار وجودند ولی

عشق داند که درین دایره سرگردانند

> Intellectuals think
> they are the
> pivot of
> the compass
> but love knows
> that they are
> the ones
> wandering on
> the periphery.

The framing of the existence of consciousness as either being on the circumference or at the pivot is largely determined by words. The art of the God-Realized poet is to uproot consciousness from the intellectual, rational circumference and to inspire and guide it to the pivot, as this pivot is the same as the wine goblet found in the lover's heart containing both the secrets of creation and Khizer's water of immortality. This pivot throughout Hafiz's poetry, also represents the state of God-realization. This is an entirely new conception of art—not so much the poet being a spiritual guide but poetry as a spiritual guide illuminating and guiding consciousness along the path from the realm of limited reason to the realm of limitless Love. It is a journey across the vast ocean of cognition, with a changing consciousness being the means of transport as Hafiz says here:

من و سفینهٔ حافظ که جز درین دریا

بضاعت سخن درفشان نمیبینم

> I will ride
> on Hafiz's ship
> for on
> this ocean
> it alone has
> as cargo
> the words
> that produce
> pearls.

This journey is synonymous with the spiritual path:

دست از مس وجود چو مردان ره بشوی

تا کیمیای عشق بیابی و زر شوی

> Like the men
> of the path
> wash your hands
> of the copper of
> existence
> so that you
> may find the

alchemy of
love and be
transformed into
gold.

The "path" is always specific to "the spiritual path" in Hafiz. It is fluctuations in the veil of poetic beauty that provide illumination along each step of it.

So the task for the God-Realized poet is to leave vocabulary in a rational context, and infuse it with a luminosity that illumines consciousness. Of course, the greater the relativity or rationality the less pure the mirror reflecting the infinite as it is the dross of the finite that darkens or clouds it. So, the context of verbal expression must ascend from the limits of the rational to the infinity of the Uncreated providing pure reflections or elegant veils along the way. Seen another way, as wine, the goblet, the tavern are all metaphors—that is, in reality they are just words and don't exist—then it is words that are providing the reflection. And as both Love and words are substanceless existences—the one being a substanceless Reality and the other a substanceless illusion— there is no reason why these two can't be welded into one, forming the perfect mirror for Love's beauty.

Obviously, the base state of consciousness on the circumference must not be ignored, for if it is, it will not be enticed to begin the journey. The God-Realized poet then has to write to this realm of the rational mind, and having captivated this consciousness—draw it to the pivot that is the abode of Love. The journey is a journey in consciousness only and the vehicle of travel is the transformation of a mundane rational definition of words into their non-rational poetic use expressing the limitless beauty of Love at creation's pivot. Looked at another way, it is a journey from the mind to the heart. Yet it is not just the elevation of higher consciousness that Hafiz is concerned with, it is just as much the elevation of the lowest. And this concern for the lowest cannot be a matter of condescension for the poetry that is anything less than fully enthralling at all levels fails in its spirituality.

Accordingly, the art of Hafiz skirts using only the elevated language that is the purview of the intellectual and spiritual elite, and also writes in a language that touches all no matter where they are. To do other than this would be to limit the rays of this poetic illumination of consciousness, and the resulting mirror that his writing creates would not reflect all of creation but just the elevated parts. This is where Hafiz's poetry succeeds beyond that of all others. To put it another way, the copper is just as important as the gold for without the copper, there is nothing to transform, and without anything to transform, there is no journey, and without a journey, there is no need for Hafiz to write.

Many may find it hard to accept that poetry could have such a transforming effect on consciousness, but during the time of Hafiz it was *the* art form. Hafiz speaks of its force here:

طی مکان ببین و زمان در سلوک شعر
کین طفل یک شبه ره یک ساله میرود

See
the speed
of poetry
traversing
space
and
time
for this
child of
one night
travels
the road
of one
year.

To fail to write to all levels of consciousness is to condition the love whose unconditional nature Hafiz is writing about, making an elevated elitism—the paradises of religion and the mind—the preserve of beauty whereas in Hafiz's art

God's limitless beauty manifests everywhere, even in the dust:

گرچه خورشید فلک چشم و چراغ عالم است
روشنای بخش چشم اوست خاک پای تو

Although the sun
of the heavens is
the light
of the world
it is the dust
of your feet
that gives
the eye
of the sun
its brightness.

بگفتمی که بها چیست خاک پایش را
گرم حیات گران مایه جاودان بودی

May I tell you the
worth of
the dust of
His feet
for it
we would sacrifice
the wealth of
eternal life.

ثواب روزه و حج قبول آن کس برد
که خاک میکده عشق را زیارت کرد

The spiritual
reward of
fasting and
pilgrimage
to Mecca
is obtained
by the one

who has
gone on
pilgrimage
to the dust
of the
wine tavern
of love.

ای نسیم سحری خاک در یار بیار
که کند حافظ از او دیدهء دل نورانی

Morning breeze
bring the
dust of
the threshold
of the
Beloved
so that
Hafiz
may
illumine the
eye of
his heart.

گنج در آستین و کیسه تهی
جام گیتی نمای و خاک رهیم

I have
the treasure
in my sleeve
but my
purse is
empty
I have the
world-revealing
cup
and
I am
the dust

of the
road.

به سر جام جم آنگه نظر توانی کرد

که خاک میکده کحل بصر توانی کرد

When you
are able
to make
the dust of
the tavern
the collyrium
of sight you'll
be able to see
the mysteries
of Jamshid's cup.

It is not just by expressing an infinite existence—and God as infinite beauty—within the ordinary and finite that makes these couplets of interest, it is also the vast metaphoric streams surging through them. Or, to put it another way, if the mirror of Jamshid's cup or the mirror of the heart contains all of creation and if Hafiz's poetry, in describing this perfect reflection, is designed to do the same then these vast concepts must appear equally within the finite.

This intention to write poetry that inspires while also skirting the rationals of the mind to touch the emotions of the heart informs Hafiz's poetry on all levels. It is this intention that is responsible for the lack of logical progressions in his poems as is seen here:

یوسف گم گشته باز آید به کنعان غم مخور

کلبهٔ احزان شود روزی گلستان غم مخور

این دل غم دیده حالش به شود دل بد مکن

وین سر شوریده باز آید به سامان غم مخور

دور گردون گر دو روزی بر مراد ما نبود

دایما یکسان نباشد کار دوران غم مخور

گر بهار عمر باشد باز بر تخت چمن
چتر گل در سرکشی ای مرغ خوشخوان غم مخور

ای دل ار سیل فنا بنیاد هستی بر کند
چون تو را نوح است کشتیبان ز طوفان غم مخور

هان مشو نومید چون واقف نه یی بر سرّ غیب
باشد اندر پرده بازی های پنهان غم مخور

در بیابان گر ز شوق کعبه خواهی زد قدم
سرزنشها گر کند خار مغیلان غم مخور

گرچه منزل بس خطرناک است و مقصد ناپدید
هیچ راهی نیست کان را نیست پایان غم مخور

حال ما در فرقت جانان و ابرام رقیب
جمله میداند خدای حال گردان غم مخور

حافظا در کنج فقر و خلوت شبهای تار
تا بود وردت دعا و درس قرآن غم مخور

Lost Joseph has returned to Caanan, don't grieve
The house of sorrow will one day become a rose
    garden, don't grieve

This heart having seen so much sorry will be repaired
this emotional upheaval with return to rest, don't
    grieve.

If for two days the revolutions of the firmament do
    not turn to our desire
the nature of their turning does not forever remain
    the same, don't grieve.

167

If the springtime of life returns the nightingale will
    sing on
the throne of the meadow under the petal of a red
    rose, don't grieve.

Heart, if the flood of annihilation uproots the
    foundation of your existence
as you have Noah as the captain of you ship, don't
    grieve.

Unaware of the secrets don't give up hope
for behind the veil many hidden games are being
    played, don't grieve.

If inspired to cross the desert on pilgrimage to Mecca
you experience the reproachful sting of thrones,
    don't grieve.

Although the path to the way-station is very
    dangerous and the destination is not seen
there is no road that does not have an end, don't
    grieve.

God knows everything about the whirling fortunes of
    our state
in separation from the Beloved and the antagonism
    of the rival, don't grieve.

Hafiz, in the corner of poverty and the dark nights of
    seclusion
So long as you pray and recite the Koran, don't
    grieve.

For the most part these couplets, being unconnected with
one another, come out of nowhere and stand in stark relief.
This is a key element to Hafiz's style. As the rational mind
is the cognitive storehouse of the relative nothing of
creation it is located on the circumference, and has no place
in the infinite uncreated reality of Love at the pivot. Yet
without using the rational mind, there can be no cognition.

Hafiz's task then is *to use the mind to write around the mind to touch the heart.* Or, to put it another way, to use cognition to write into a realm beyond cognition—to form a poetic bridge from illusion to Reality. This style is in sync with the Koranic mystical conception of Ruzi-alast—literary, "the day in pre-eternity." This is the conception that the manifestation of creation is happening in the "eternal Now" with each element independently coming into creation from a timeless origin. In the same way, this non-logical style in Hafiz's poems in combination with his development of a torrent of images—these images permeating the limited rational by having been given oceanic associations—produce an immense impact, as all unexpectedly come out of nowhere there being no logical sequence heralding their arrival. The poetic beat of rhythm and rhyme only enhance the impact of each couplet as another vast unexpected symbol or image springs into existence, aimed with great skill at the heart of the lover, hitting on a downbeat at impact. Essentially, these couplets are crafted as arrows carrying the poison of love's infinity slaying the confining, limited, illusions within:

تیر عاشق کش ندانم بر دل حافظ که زد
این قدر دانم که از شعر ترش خون میچکید

> I don't know
> who shot the
> lover-killing arrow
> into Hafiz's heart;
> all I know is
> that blood drips
> from his fresh verse.

In this sense, the tongue of his poetry becomes the craftsman, using its elegant beauty to craft a corresponding beauty in the existence of the reader.

To enhance this journey, Hafiz calls for a saturation in the beauty of nature, as it is the forces of nature that have produced the crowning achievement of creation—not just a human consciousness but a human consciousness with

169

the ability to have deep insights into the nature of God. Hafiz places the value of these experiences of natural beauty above those of learning or scholarship as he sees the accumulation of knowledge as something that enhances the ego, dulls insight and keeps consciousness attached to the periphery:

ای دل به هر ز ه دانش و عمرت ز دست رفت
صد مایه داشتیِّ و نکردی کفایتی

Oh heart
you had
a hundred things
going for you but
you wasted your
life pursuing the
triflings of
knowledge
instead of gaining
a permanent
quality.

حافظ رسید موسم گل معرفت مگوی
دریاب نقد وقت وز چون و چرا مپرس

Hafiz it
is the
season of
the rose
don't speak
of divine
knowledge;
drown in
the moment
and don't
question
why and
wherefore.

As I mentioned, Love is an uncreated force without relativity so there is no friction in it meaning that it is ultimately the only force that exists, as all others, possessing relativity, from the frictional force of this relativity will dissolve into nothing. However, for the carving and cutting of a new, infinite individuality, Love needs the friction of relativity, and in Love's hand this becomes the tool for crafting the unique individuality of Love's lover. Hafiz presents that all of the suffering and striving that Love experiences in an individual form in separation is from this cutting and crafting. And, as the lover strives to lose himself in the Beloved, the forces of the relativity of creation intensify and the rate of crafting increases, until his uniqueness reaches a carved perfection.

In all of his writing Hafiz presents the Beloved as having a double-faceted difficulty—how to maintain a separation that allows Him to express and experience His true nature as Love; and how to achieve the Union between lover and Beloved that His existence as infinite Love demands. This dual nature of God's primary desire to create separation along with His desire to express unconditional Love by reuniting with His lover, creates not just the "push and pull" of the lover-Beloved relationship, but also the constant "push and pull" that gives creation and all of life its vibrancy. As Hafiz presents it, it is only through the conditioning of the unconditional that the separation necessary for lover and Beloved to exist is created. Having created this, it is only through God's expression of His unconditional Love that the conditioning He initially created is removed. Seen another way, God's need to express His unconditional Love prevents Him from doing just that, as the full expression of unconditional love annihilates all of the conditions producing separation leaving no one for God's to express His unconditional love to. Simply, God has to have veils of relative darkness to become aware of His own light. Hafiz's own spiritual journey takes him to this veilless existence of God and, in discovering that there is nothing to be seen, finds all else is revealed:

حسن روی تو به یک جلوه که در آینه کرد
این همه نقش در آینهٔ اوهم افتاد

The beauty
of your face
with the burst
of one ray of
splendor reflected
all of these forms
in the mirror
of imagination.

    Finally, the difference between east and west is that the east has benefitted from a number of God-realized poets crafting language into a spiritual awakener and guide, whereas the west does not appear to have had any of these souls. As there are many similarities between the religions of east and west such as the "Good thoughts, good words, good deeds" precepts of Zoroastrianism, the Christian Golden Rule, and the Hindu Law of Karma, this poetic use of language to create a spiritual vocabulary within a rational one appears to be the major difference between these two worlds, as this transformation creates an entire dynamic of cognition largely missing in the west. This is the genius of the east, most specifically the Persian language, and most exceptionally Hafiz as he presents himself as the supreme artist, accepting the appellation of "La alsani ghab," literally, the tongue revealing the hidden mysteries of God.

    There is a measure to Hafiz's great poetic achievement, and that is the effect it has had on the other literary traditions of the east. Although the other literary traditions were well-established and pre-dating him by centuries, Hafiz's poetry flooded all with his lyrics being sung from the shores of the Euphrates to the heights of India's Deccan plateau. Even today the vocabulary of love in these regions has a strong mystical flavor from his revelatory writings. His artistry was poured over in the west as well, where generations of writers hungry for a poetic vocabulary containing the mysteries of existence devoured his work. In fact, his work was first translated into English as early as 1771 by William Jones. It would leave a mark on such Western writers as Thoreau, Goethe, and Ralph Waldo Emerson (the last referred to him as "a poet's poet") to mention just a few. In our time, too, a new generation inspired by hints of spiritual unfoldment is in search of the mysteries revealed in the writings of this incomparable genius. All of this is to be expected for as Hafiz says:

من که ره بردم به گنج حسن بی پایان دوس
صد گدای همچو خود را بعد از ین قارون کنم

Having traveled
the path to the
Beloved's treasury
of limitless
beauty; I will
turn a hundred
beggars like me
into Korahs.[9]

Or:

چو زر عزیز وجود است نظم من آری
قبول دولتیان کیمیای این مس شد

My verse is
the crowning
gold of creation;
the great ones
acknowledge
the alchemy of
this cooper.

And finally:

---

[9] Korah is Croesus the king of Lydia (560 B.C.) who was defeated by Cyrus the Great of Persia in 546 B.C., renowned in Greek and Persian culture for his great wealth.

در قلم آورد حافظ قصه لعل لبت
آب حیوان میرود هر دم ز اقلامم هنوز

Hafiz brought
into his pen
the story of
your ruby lip
now from it
flows the
water of
eternal
life.

LINES ON BEAUTY

Nicola Masciandaro

> One day when I was at prayer, He was pleased
> to show me His hands only; their beauty was
> beyond description.
>
> — Teresa of Avila

> Beauty is love kissing horror.
>
> — Ladislav Klima

> I like beauty in everything; but what is beauty?
> The beauty that never perishes, that is immortal,
> is real beauty . . . As it is, you do not love beauty
> but dirt, because you yourselves are unclean.
> Get rid of your own foulness and then find out
> what beauty is!
>
> — Meher Baba

Who can write about beauty? The beautiful, maybe, but
beauty—that is too much. I am afraid to do so. So being
afraid, I will hide and repeat myself, sharing here only a
few lines on beauty which I have already written:

The one who has seen beauty | Is no longer I | For that is
its true duty | To pierce through your lie.

Why you are afraid to see the source of beauty.

Unwitnessable face-to-face | Pure asymmetry | Most tragic rift in time and space | Emerald beauty.

It is called truth, love, beauty, and silence / Because no words express this violence.

Alien shock of beauty | Color from beyond | New spark of ancient duty | Our all-breaking bond.

Beauty lives where there is nothing to live for.

Beauty misdrew her image | By thinking of it | Now her wings look like a cage | And her smile a bit.

The only explanation is beauty.

I walk among nothing | In beauty never fed | Down pathways of splendor | Without mouth or head.

The irresistible beauty of someone who is neither oneself nor someone else.

Life weeps eternal at your tomb | Dying of beauty | Seeing everywhere is no room | For this endless sea.

To lose myself in the beauty that no one will ever know you have.

To see light falling slower | Than a single thought | To know Beauty as knower | Of all things and naught.

Bask in beauty until your beheading is beheaded.

Intelligence will never fathom the source of beauty.

Fire embrace of lighting arms | Burning to zero | Pure beauty beyond all charms | Love with no hero.

To become something whose head Beauty asks to be brought on a platter. #success

Your beauty is pure zero | Nothing but the all | Still bleeding from an arrow | Shot through my eyeball.

Because you are very beautiful, it is very good that it is not your beauty.

To die trapped inside a beauty you cannot see.

Coppa del Universo, final score: Beauty 1, All Else 0.

The beauty of infinite universes proceeding without oneself.

No one is tired enough – the beauty of someone who is tired enough.

Become such a beautiful monster that your desires run in fear.

That there is beauty is more beautiful than any beauty.

To beautifully forget all about beauty in the midst of it.

Kaf means *palm* in Arabic, Cuneiform, Farsi, Hebrew, Phoenician, Urdu, and many other languages. **Kaf** is the letter K in each. It signifies touch, vulnerability, intimacy. The hand lifted before it is clenched.

Kaf shares its name with mount Qaf, the fabled goal of the Hoopoe and its followers in the Sufi poem The Conference of the Birds. It is half of **Kaf**ka, the Czech author of empirical impasse, cruel absurdity. Like the Hoopoe and **Kaf**ka's K, we travel by wandering, without preconceived destination.

Kaf is an inquiry into the very possibility of itself, as well as a sustained meditation on the political, geographic and cultural borders that obscure this possibility.

www.kafcollective.com

Made in the USA
Middletown, DE
22 July 2018